# JANICE VANCLEAVE'S
# Super Science
# Models

John Wiley & Sons, Inc.

Published by John Wiley & Sons, Inc., Hoboken, New Jersey
Published simultaneously in Canada

Design and production by Navta Associates, Inc.

The publisher and the author have made every reasonable effort to ensure that the experiments and activities in this book are safe when conducted as instructed but assume no responsibility for any damage caused or sustained while performing the experiments or activities in the book. Parents, guardians, and/or teachers should supervise young readers who undertake the experiments and activities in this book.

For general information about our other products and services, please contact our Customer Care Department within the United States at (800) 762-2974, outside the United States at (317) 572-3993 or fax (317) 572-4002.

Wiley also publishes its books in a variety of electronic formats. Some content that appears in print may not be available in electronic books. For more information about Wiley products, visit our web site at www.wiley.com.

***Library of Congress Cataloging-in-Publication Data***

VanCleave, Janice Pratt.
  Janice VanCleave's super science models/Janice VanCleave.
          p. cm.
  Includes index.
  ISBN 0-471-25221-2 (pbk. : alk. paper)
  1.Mathematical models.   I. Title: Super science models.  II. Title.
  QA401.V36  2004
  502.2' 8—dc22                                    2004002224

Printed in the United States of America

10  9  8  7  6  5  4  3  2  1

# Dedication

It is my pleasure to dedicate this book to a model husband.
My helpmate: Wade VanCleave

# Acknowledgments

A special note of gratitude to these educators who assisted by pretesting the activities and/or by providing scientific information—the elementary education students of Dr. Nancy Cherry, instructor, Lamburth University, Jackson, Tennessee: Brandy Clement, Susan Crownover, Kendra Edwards, Amity Freytag, Holli Helms, Laticia Hicks, Nikki Keener, Jodie Leach, Kristen Malone, Karrinn Penrod, Brandi Phillips, Glenda Raven, Bridget Smith, and Krista Vaughn.

# Contents

# Introduction

So you want to make a science model. Great! You'll get to show off your work to your class, and you may even get an award for your science project. But the best part is that you'll learn a lot about science by investigating and sharing what you have learned with others.

Scientists often use models to make it easier to describe things. A **model** is a representation of an object or system, including diagrams and three-dimensional structures. Some models are larger than the object they represent, such as a cell model. Other models are smaller than the objects they represent, such as a model of the solar system.

This book presents fun model ideas on a wide variety of subjects such as astronomy, biology, chemistry, earth science, and physics. If you thumb through the book, you'll get ideas of how some of the models are presented. The basic method for presenting a model described in one chapter, as well as the information in the appendixes, can be used to present other topics. For example, one chapter uses tab books to display information about telescopes, but tab books are also useful in displaying information about other topics. In the 25 main chapters, you'll find facts about the subject of the model, ideas for other models, as well as ideas on how to display your model. The 12 appendixes in the book explain different presentation techniques, from tab books to backboards, that can be used for many different types of projects. It's your job to pick a topic and to develop the model ideas into your own terrific model.

## HOW TO USE THIS BOOK

You can start anywhere in the book. Flip through the chapters for a topic that sounds interesting. Begin your model project by reading the selected chapter completely. Then collect all the materials needed for the model and follow the procedures carefully. The format for each chapter is as follows:

- **Make a Model of:** A statement introducing the topic of the model. This statement is followed by science information about the model topic.

- **Activity:** An activity that provides information for developing a basic model on the topic being studied. Each activity includes a **Purpose,** which identifies the model to be made, a complete list of easy-to-find **Materials,** step-by-step **Procedures,** a section identifying the expected **Results,** and a **Why?** section that provides specific information about the model.

- **On Your Own!:** Additional fun model activities relating to the topic and/or display ideas. Many of the display ideas refer to instructions provided in the appendixes.

- **Book List:** A list of other science books about the topic.

# I

# ASTRONOMY

SOLAR SYSTEM

SUN

Jupiter

Saturn

Uranus

Neptune

# Line Up

### *Make a Model of the Solar System!*

**Celestial bodies** are natural things in the sky, such as **stars** (bodies made of gases that are so hot they give off light), **planets** (bodies that revolve around a sun and shine only by the light they reflect), and **moons** (bodies that revolve around planets and shine only by the light they reflect). **Revolve** or **orbit** means to move in a curved path around another body. The curved path one celestial body takes around another is also called an orbit. A **solar system** is a group of celestial bodies that revolve around a central body that is a star called a **sun.**

The bodies that orbit our Sun include **minor planets** (small rocky bodies mainly between the orbits of Mars and Jupiter; also called **asteroids**), nine **major planets** (planets with diameters larger than Ceres, the largest asteroid) and their moons, **comets** (bodies of dust, gases, and ice that move in an extremely elongated path), and space debris.

The major planets in order from the Sun are Mercury, Venus, Earth, Mars, Jupiter, Saturn,

Uranus, Neptune, and Pluto. One way to remember the order of the planets is to remember the sentence, My Very Eager Mother Just Served Us Nice Pizza. (The first letter of each word is the first letter of the name of each planet in order from the Sun.) The diagram shows the planets in order from the Sun but does not represent their distance.

The **universe** is Earth and everything else in space. Early models of the universe were **geocentric** (Earth-centered). The Greek astronomer Aristotle (384–322 B.C.) supported the geocentric view, and his ideas about the universe were considered true by most people for almost 2,000 years. Ptolemy (87–165), an influential Roman astronomer, agreed with Aristotle's geocentric view. No one seriously questioned Ptolemy's theory until 1543, when the Polish astronomer Nicolaus Copernicus (1473–1543) published a book suggesting a **heliocentric** (Sun-centered) model. The Italian scientist Galileo Galilei (1564–1642) agreed with Copernicus's view that the Sun was the

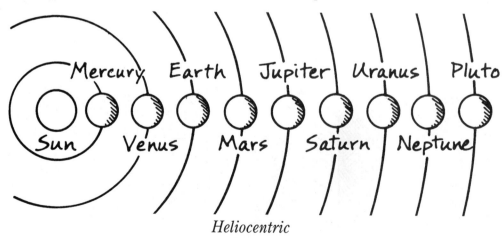

*Heliocentric*

Mercury and Venus are called **inferior planets** because their orbits are closer than Earth's orbit to the Sun. Mercury is the smallest inferior planet and the one closest to the Sun. It orbits the Sun once in about 88 Earth days. (An **Earth day** is about 24 hours and is the time it takes Earth to **rotate,** or turn about its **axis**—the imaginary line through the center of a body about which the body rotates.) Venus is the second planet from the Sun. It orbits the Sun in 225 Earth days. Venus is generally the easiest planet to see in the sky and shines more brightly than any star.

The planets whose orbits are farther than Earth's orbit from the Sun are called **superior planets.** The superior planets include Mars, Jupiter, Saturn, Uranus, Neptune, and Pluto. Mars is called the red planet because of its reddish glow. The red color is due to the rusty iron in its soil. Mars orbits the Sun in 1.9 Earth years. (An **Earth year** is the time it takes Earth to orbit around the Sun, or about 365 days.)

Jupiter is the largest planet. It is made mostly of gases and has a storm in its **atmosphere** (the blanket of gas surrounding a celestial body) that looks like a red spot. This spot is larger than the Earth. It takes 11.9 Earth years for Jupiter to orbit the Sun.

Saturn is 9.4 times larger than Earth. It is the most distant planet that is relatively easily viewed in the sky without a telescope. Through a telescope, rings can be viewed around Saturn. It takes 29.5 Earth years for Saturn to orbit the Sun.

Uranus is four times larger than Earth. It can be seen with the naked eye if conditions are right. It looks like a faint star. It was the first planet to be discovered through a telescope. It takes 84 Earth years for Uranus to orbit the Sun.

Neptune is almost four times as large as Earth. The German astronomer Johann Galle (1812–1910) first observed this planet through a telescope in 1846. It takes 164.8 Earth years for Neptune to orbit the Sun.

Pluto is about one-fourth as large as Earth. The American astronomer Percival Lowell (1855–1916) predicted that Pluto existed, and in 1930 the American astronomer Clyde William Tombaugh (1906–1997) found Pluto near that position. It takes Pluto 247.7 Earth years to orbit the Sun.

center of the universe. But it wasn't until the end of the 1600s that the heliocentric model was generally accepted by astronomers. Today it is known that our solar system is a very tiny part of a **galaxy** (a group of millions of stars, gas, dust, and other celestial bodies) called the Milky Way. This galaxy is just one of many galaxies in the universe. It is also known that our Sun is not in the center of the universe, only the center of our solar system.

## ACTIVITY: PLANET ORDER

### Purpose

To make a model of the order and relative sizes of the planets in our solar system.

## Materials

two 22-by-28-inch (55-by-70-cm) pieces of
   blue poster board
glue
yardstick (meterstick)
drawing compass
pen
2 sheets of 9-by-12-inch (22.5-by-30-cm)
   construction paper—1 orange, 1 white
scissors
two black markers—1 wide-point,
   1 fine-point
metric ruler
pencil
two 22-by-28-inch (55-by-70-cm) pieces of
   white poster board
square of white poster board
9 different colored crayons—1 blue, 1 red,
   and 7 other colors except yellow
transparent tape
string

## Procedure

1. Use the blue poster board to make a narrow three-paneled backboard with a title strip, using the instructions in Appendix 1, Part A.

2. Using the compass, draw a large semicircle (with 8" diameter) on the orange construction paper. Also draw long, thin (4") triangles to represent rays of sunlight. Cut out the semicircle and triangles. Use the wide-point marker to label the curved figure "Sun." Glue the Sun and light rays to the left panel of the backboard, as shown.

3. Fold the white construction paper in half two times. Draw four stars on the folded paper. Cut out the stars, cutting through all four layers of paper. Glue the stars to the center and right panels of the backboard.

4. Use the wide-point marker to label the title strip of the backboard "Solar System."

5. Use the ruler and pencil to draw a 1½-inch (3.75-cm) square on the white poster board. Cut out the square and use it to trace four more squares on the white poster board. Cut out the four squares.

6. Draw a circle of about 0.2 cm diameter in the center of each side of one poster board square. Label both sides of the poster board square "Pluto."

7. Repeat step 6 using the remaining poster board squares for each of the planets in the following table.

| Planet Model Sizes | |
|---|---|
| **Planet Name** | **Diameter of Model** |
| Pluto | 0.2 cm |
| Mercury | 0.5 cm |
| Mars | 0.7 cm |
| Venus | 1.2 cm |
| Earth | 1.3 cm |

8. On the remaining poster board, use the compass to draw a 5-cm–diameter circle. Cut out the circle and label both sides of the circle "Uranus."

9. Using the sizes in the following table, repeat step 8 to make circles for each of the remaining planets.

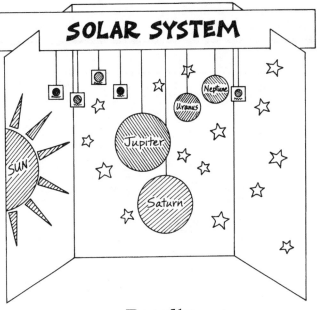

## SOLAR SYSTEM

| Planet Model Sizes | |
|---|---|
| **Planet Name** | **Diameter of Model** |
| Uranus | 5 cm |
| Neptune | 5 cm |
| Saturn | 12 cm |
| Jupiter | 12 cm |

10. Using the blue crayon, color the circles on the front and back of the square for planet Earth. Color the circle for Mars red. Use the remaining crayons to color the remaining seven planet models whatever you like.

11. Cut two 16-inch (35-cm) pieces of string. Tape one piece of string apiece to the tops of the Jupiter and Saturn models.

12. Cut seven 10-inch (25-cm) pieces of string. Tape each piece of string to the top of each of the remaining planet models.

13. With the title strip in place on the backboard, attach the free ends of the strings to the title strip so the models start at 6 inches (15 cm) from the left bottom edge of the title strip and are spaced 2 inches (10 cm) apart in this order from the left: Mercury, Venus, Earth, Mars, Jupiter, Saturn, Uranus, Neptune, Pluto.

14. Adjust the lengths of the strings so that the planet models do not overlap, making some strings longer than others.

### Results

You have made a model of the relative sizes of the planets in their order from the Sun.

### Why?

The model represents the known planets in order from the Sun. While it does show the relative sizes of the planets, it does not represent the actual distance between them.

## LAYERED BOOK

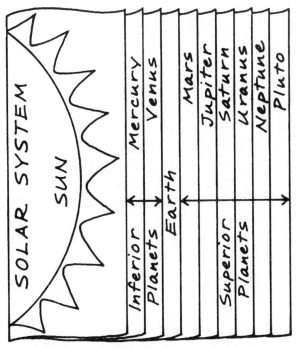

| | | | | Planet Facts and Figures | | | |
|---|---|---|---|---|---|---|---|
| Celestial Body | Diameter, miles (km) | Average Density g/ml (water = 1) | Albedo | Aphelion or Greatest Distance from Sun, millions of miles (millions of km) | Perihelion or Least Distance from Sun, millions of miles (millions of km) | Average Distance from Sun, millions of miles (millions of km) | Period of Rotation, hours |
| Mercury | 3,047 (4,878) | 5.4 | 0.1 | 44 (70) | 29 (46) | 36 (58) | 1,407.5 |
| Venus | 7,562 (12,100) | 5.3 | 0.76 | 68 (109) | 67 (107) | 68 (108) | 5,832 |
| Earth | 7,973 (12,757) | 5.5 | 0.39 | 95 (152) | 92 (147) | 93 (149) | 24 |
| Mars | 4,247 (6,796) | 3.9 | 0.16 | 156 (249) | 129 (207) | 143 (228) | 24.6 |
| Jupiter | 89,875 (143,800) | 1.3 | 0.52 | 510 (816) | 463 (741) | 486 (778) | 9.8 |
| Saturn | 75,412 (120,660) | 0.7 | 0.61 | 942 (1,507) | 842 (1,347) | 892 (1,427) | 10.2 |
| Uranus | 31,949 (51,118) | 1.2 | 0.35 | 1,875 (3,000) | 1,712 (2,740) | 1,794 (2,870) | 15.2 |
| Neptune | 30,937 (49,500) | 1.7 | 0.35 | 2,838 (4,540) | 2,782 (4,452) | 2,810 (4,497) | 16 |
| Pluto | 1,434 (2,294) | 2.0 | 0.5 | 4,604 (7,366) | 2,771 (4,434) | 3,688 (5,900) | 153 |

## ON YOUR OWN

Another way to make a model of the solar system is with a layered book. This book can be made using five sheets of different colored copy or construction paper and the instructions in Appendix 2, Part C.

In the layered solar system book, include facts you find in your research as well as facts from the introduction to this chapter and those listed in the table shown, "Planet Facts and Figures."

## BOOK LIST

Becklake, Sue. *Space: The Official Planetarium Book.* Rocklin, Calif.: Prima, 1994. A journey through the solar system, including a study of the planets in our solar system.

Snowden, Sheila. *The Young Astronomer.* London: Usborne, 1989. A guide to introduce beginners to the study of the heavens, including the study of the planets and their order in the solar system.

VanCleave, Janice. *Janice VanCleave's Solar System.* New York: Wiley, 2000. Experiments about the order of the planets and other solar system topics. Each chapter contains ideas that can be turned into award-winning science fair projects.

# Lighted Side
## *Make a Model of the Moon's Phases!*

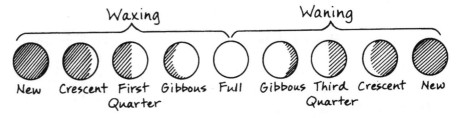

Waxing | Waning

New | Crescent | First Quarter | Gibbous | Full | Gibbous | Third Quarter | Crescent | New

The Moon's shape appears to change from day to day. These repeating shapes of the sunlit surface of the Moon facing Earth are called **moon phases.** Phases are seen because the Moon revolves around Earth as the Earth/Moon system revolves around the Sun. Just as half of Earth has daylight and the other half nighttime, about half of the Moon is lighted by the Sun while the other half is not lighted. The phases of the Moon depend on how much of the sunlit half can be seen from Earth at any one time.

The relative position of the Moon to the Sun changes daily. The farther the Moon is from the Sun in the Moon's orbit around Earth, the more of the lighted side we see. When the Moon is opposite the Sun with Earth in between but not blocking the Sun's light, the side of the Moon facing Earth is lighted. This phase is called a **full moon.** When the Moon is between Earth and the Sun, the lighted side faces away from Earth and the side facing Earth is not illuminated. This phase is called a **new moon.** When the Moon is in between these two positions, different fractions of the lighted side are seen. The time it takes the Moon to revolve around Earth and to go through all of its phases is about 29 days and is called a **lunar month.**

Following the new moon, more and more of the Moon's lighted side is visible and the phases are said to be **waxing** (getting bigger). The first part of the lighted side is seen about 24 hours after the new moon phase. This phase

is called the **crescent** phase and looks like a small, curved section with pointed ends. In about seven days after the new moon, half of the side of the Moon facing Earth is lighted. This is the first quarter phase, called such because about one-fourth of a lunar month has passed. The next phase is **gibbous,** which has more lighted area than the first quarter phase, but less than the full moon phase.

Following the full moon, the Moon goes through the same phases in reverse. These phases are said to be **waning** (getting smaller). The waning phases are gibbous, **third quarter** (when half of the side of the Moon facing Earth is lighted and three-fourths of a lunar month has passed), and crescent. Then the cycle begins again with the new moon.

## ACTIVITY: MOON PHASES

### Purpose

To model the Moon's phases.

### Materials

12 sheets of 9-by-12-inch (22.5-by-30-cm)
    construction paper—6 black, 6 white
scissors
2 to 3 sheets of newspaper

glue

pen

protractor

two 3-by-5-inch (7.5-by-12.5-cm) white
unlined index cards

drawing compass

4 sheets of white copy paper

black crayon

## Procedure

1. Fold each sheet of construction paper in half
by placing the short sides together.

2. Unfold the sheets of paper.

3. Lay the newspaper on a table to protect the
table.

4. Place one sheet of white construction paper
on the newspaper.

5. Glue the left half of one of the black sheets
over the right half of the white sheet. Then
glue the left half of a second white sheet
over the right half of the black sheet, as
shown.

6. Continue gluing the sheets of construction
paper together, alternating between black
and white until you end up with the right
side of a white page. You will have a black
piece of paper left over.

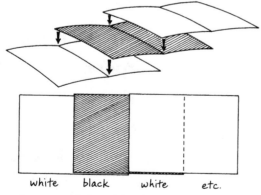

white    black    white    etc.

7. Cut the remaining black sheet in half along
the crease.

8. Glue one of the half pieces of black paper
over the right side of the last sheet of
white paper.

9. Turn the glued papers over and glue the
other half piece of black paper over the
right side of the first sheet of white paper.

10. Allow the glue to dry, then fold the pages
accordion style.

11. On one of the white
index cards, use the pen
and the protractor to
draw a diagram of the
waxing moon phases,
showing the positions of
the Moon, Earth, and the
Sun, like the one shown
here. Label the card
"Waxing Moon Phases."

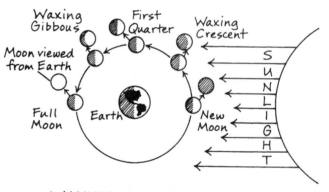

WAXING MOON PHASES

12. Glue the index card with the waxing
phases to the first black section of construction paper.

13. Use the compass to draw five 4-inch
(10-cm) –diameter circles on the white
copy paper.

14. Use the black crayon to color the
unlighted parts of the five waxing phases
on the circles, as shown in the figure at
the beginning of this chapter, page 9.

**15.** Cut out the circles and glue them, in order of the phases, to the remaining five black sections.

**16.** With the paper model lying flat on the table and the full moon on the right, turn the model over. Do this by picking up the right end and flipping it to the left. The moon phases should be on the bottom of the model with the full moon under the left end.

**17.** Repeat steps 12 and 13 to show the position of Earth, the Sun, and the Moon during the waning phases of the Moon.

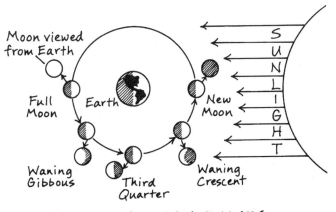

WANING MOON PHASES

**18.** Repeat steps 13 through 15, using the waning phases.

**19.** Fold the sections accordion style and press to crease the folds. Then open and stand on one edge to display the phases.

## Results

You have made a model of the waxing and waning phases of the moon.

## Why?

In the Northern Hemisphere, during the waxing phases of the Moon, the lighted part of the moon is on the right. But during the waning phases, the remaining lighted part is on the left. Thus in the Northern Hemisphere you can tell if the Moon's phases are waxing or waning, since the waning phases are the part of the Moon that is "left," as in remaining, and they are on the left side of the Moon.

## ON YOUR OWN!

You can add information about each of the diagrams represented on your model. Do this by writing directly on the white page opposite each diagram, or write on colored index cards and glue them to the white pages. At the top, put the name of the diagram represented on the opposite black page. Underneath that, you can include other information about the diagram.

## BOOK LIST

Moran, Stephen P. Astronomy for Dummies. New York: Wiley, 1999. A fun, fact-filled guide.

Pasachoff, Jay M. Peterson First Guide to Astronomy. New York: Houghton Mifflin, 1988. A simplified field guide to the stars, the planets, and the universe with information about the Moon's phases.

VanCleave, Janice. Janice VanCleave's Solar System. New York: Wiley, 2000. Experiments about Moon phases and other solar system topics. Each chapter contains ideas that can be turned into award-winning science fair projects.

# 3

# Lookers

## *Make a Model of a Telescope!*

No one knows who first put together the right combination of lenses to make the first **telescope** (an instrument used to make distant objects appear nearer and larger). One story is that some children playing in an Amsterdam optical shop owned by the Dutch spectacle-maker Hans Lippershey (c.1570–1619) happened to look through two lenses at the same time and saw an amazing magnified world. Another story is that Lippershey himself made the discovery. In any case, Lippershey improved on the discovery by putting two lenses in a tube, one at each end. He called the invention a "looker," and he sold them in his shop. Lippershey's looker made it possible to view distant objects.

The Italian astronomer Galileo Galilei (1564–1642) is often given credit for the invention of the telescope, as well as for being the first person to study the sky with the instrument. Galileo didn't invent the telescope, but he did make improvements to it. And Galileo may not have been the first to use a telescope to observe the sky, but he was the first to report many astronomical discoveries, such as the fact that Jupiter has moons.

In a Galilean telescope, the **objective lens** (the lens at the end of a telescope pointed toward an object being viewed) was **concave** (curved inward, like the surface of a plate). The **eyepiece** (the lens of a telescope that one looks through) was **convex** (curved outward, like the surface of a ball). This lens combination provided an enlarged, upright **image** (the likeness of an object formed by a lens or a mirror). The Keplerian telescope was invented in 1611 by the German astronomer Johannes Kepler (1571–1630). It used two convex lenses, which provided greater magnification than a Galilean telescope, but the image was upside-down. (A telescope that uses only lenses to make distant objects appear closer is called a **refracting telescope**).

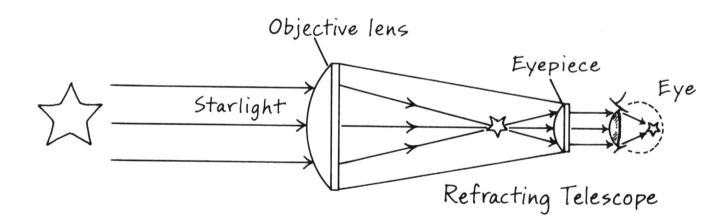

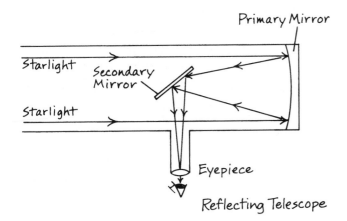

Primary Mirror

Starlight

Secondary Mirror

Starlight

Eyepiece

Reflecting Telescope

In 1721, Isaac Newton (1642–1727) improved the design of the telescope by using a combination of mirrors and a lens. This is called a **reflecting telescope** (a telescope that uses lenses and mirrors to make distant objects appear closer) or a **Newtonian telescope.** Today the largest telescopes on Earth are the Keck telescopes in Hawaii, which are reflecting telescopes with an aperture of about 33 feet (10 m). **Aperture** is the diameter of the light collecting lens in a refracting telescope or the primary mirror in a reflecting telescope. The Hubble Space Telescope (HST), with an aperture of about 8 feet (2.4 m), is a reflecting telescope that orbits Earth. It was launched on April 25, 1990, and is used to observe distant objects in space. The Hubble is scheduled to be replaced in the near future.

white butcher paper

cardboard box with at least two 11-by-16-inch (27.5-by-40-cm) sides

1 sheet of light-colored copy paper (yellow works well, but you can use any light color)

pencil

ruler

fine-tip black marker

glue stick

## Procedure

1. Using the scissors and tape, wrap the box with the butcher paper so that one of the 11-by-16 inch (27.5-by-40-cm) or larger sides has a smooth covering.

2. On the sheet of colored paper, use the pencil and ruler to draw a refracting telescope, using the figure here for reference and labeling these parts: (1) Light from a distant object, (2) Objective Lens, (3) Refracted Light Ray, (4) First Image, (5) Eyepiece, (6) Second Image.

3. Draw a face on the paper so that it looks like an eye is looking through the eyepiece of the telescope.

4. Draw a crescent Moon at the end of the telescope opposite the face.

## ACTIVITY: REFRACTING TELESCOPE

### Purpose

To make a model of a refracting telescope.

### Materials

transparent tape
scissors

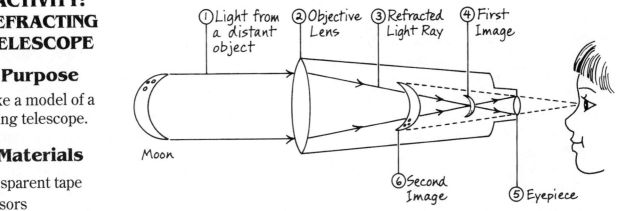

① Light from a distant object  ② Objective Lens  ③ Refracted Light Ray  ④ First Image

Moon

⑥ Second Image  ⑤ Eyepiece

5. Trace over the diagram with the black marker. Note that parts 4 and 6, first and second image, are upside-down and backward views of the actual moon.

6. Trim the edges of the colored paper so that the diagram fills most of the paper.

7. On the box use the marker to write the title "Refracting Telescope."

8. Glue the telescope diagram beneath the title.

## Results

You have made a model of a refracting telescope.

## Why?

Astronomers use telescopes to view celestial bodies. Because some celestial bodies are so far away, their light has spread out so much by the time it reaches Earth that seeing them with the naked eye is difficult or impossible. The size of the eye limits the amount of light that it can gather. But a telescope has a larger light-gathering lens, so celestial bodies that otherwise could not be seen are visible through a telescope.

The model of the telescope that you made represents a simple refracting telescope with two convex lenses: the objective lens and the eyepiece lens. The objective lens gathers light from distant objects and forms a small upside-down and backward image in front of the eyepiece lens. The eyepiece lens magnifies the image, forming the second enlarged image. The larger the objective lens, the greater the light-gathering power and the clearer and sharper the first image. The more curved the eyepiece lens, the more it magnifies the second image.

## ON YOUR OWN!

Another way to display information about each labeled part of the telescope is with tab books. Make six small tab books from 3-by-5-inch (7.5-by-12.5-cm) unlined yellow index cards. (See Appendix 3, Part A, for instructions on making small tab books.) Number the outside of the tab books from 1 through 6. Inside each tab book write information about the parts of the telescope being represented, including the following:

1. Light rays from a distant object enter the objective lens parallel to each other.

2. An objective lens is the main lens of a telescope. This lens gathers light from distant objects. Light passing through this lens is **refracted** (bent).

3. The refracted light from the objective lens is bent toward a point called the **focal point** (the point where light rays passing through a lens meet) of the lens.

4. The first image of the distant object is formed by the objective lens. This image is small and rotated 180° from the position of the object, thus the image is upside-down.

**5.** The eyepiece lens is a smaller lens that magnifies the first image, forming a second image.

**6.** The second image is a magnified version of the first image.

Once the tab books have been prepared, glue them to the box below the telescope model.

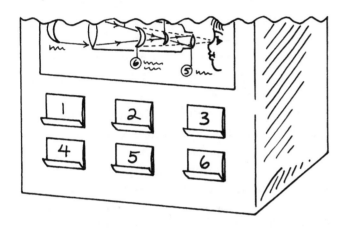

## BOOK LIST

Matloff, Gregory. *Telescope Power.* New York: Wiley, 1993. Information about telescopes, including fun activities and projects.

Schultz, Ron, et al. *Looking Inside Telescopes and the Night Sky* (X-Ray Vision). Santa Fe, N. Mex.: John Muir Publishing, 1993. A description of different kinds of telescopes, how they work, and what they tell us about the universe.

Scott, Elaine. *Close Encounters: Exploring the Universe with the Hubble Space Telescope.* New York: Disney Press, 1998. Explains what scientists have learned about our solar system and the universe from information collected by the Hubble Space Telescope.

VanCleave, Janice. *Janice VanCleave's Science through the Ages.* Hoboken, N.J.: Wiley, 2002. Fun facts and experiments about science past and present, including information about telescopes.

# 4

# Around and Around

## *Make a Model of Constellations!*

Most of the stars, the Sun, and the Moon appear to rise daily above the **horizon** (a line where the sky seems to meet Earth) in the eastern sky, and set below the horizon in the western sky. Actually, none of the celestial bodies is moving across the sky. Instead, Earth rotates, which means to turn about its axis once in about 24 hours. This movement causes the stars to appear to move overhead when viewed by an observer on Earth.

The north end of Earth's axis is called the **North Pole** and the south end is called the **South Pole**. The **equator** is an imaginary line midway between the North and South Poles. It divides Earth into two parts, the **Northern Hemisphere** (area north of the equator) and the **Southern Hemisphere** (area south of the equator). The end of the axis at the North Pole points very close to a star called **Polaris,** or the **North Star.**

What stars you see in the sky depends on where you are on Earth. When you look at the sky at night, you see only the stars that are above the horizon. These are about half of the stars that are visible to the naked eye from the observer's location. Below the horizon is another set of stars. Stars that are always above the horizon from a given location in the Northern Hemisphere are called **northern circumpolar stars.** These stars never set, but seem to go round and round Polaris without dipping below the horizon. From the North Pole, Polaris would be directly overhead and all stars in the sky above the Northern Hemisphere would be circumpolar.

**Constellations** are groups of stars that appear to make patterns in the sky. Constellations in the Northern Hemisphere that contain northern circumpolar stars are called **northern circumpolar constellations.** These constellations are always above the horizon and seem to rotate around Polaris. As one moves from the North Pole toward the equator, Polaris appears at an angle above the horizon equal to the **latitude** (the distance in degrees north and south of the equator, which is at 0° latitude) of the observer. The closer one is to the equator, the fewer circumpolar stars one sees. From the equator, Polaris is not visible and there are no circumpolar stars; here all stars rise in the east and set in the west each day.

Earth's movements also affect what stars you see. Earth not only rotates on its axis, but also changes position in the sky in relation to the stars as it revolves around the Sun. Earth's movement around the Sun causes a slight change in the part of the sky seen each day. This results in different stars being visible during each season. But Earth's North Pole continues to point toward Polaris, so the northern circumpolar stars at a given location remain the same.

+ ZENITH

DRACO

THE BIG DIPPER

URSA MINOR

URSA MAJOR    Polaris    CEPHEUS

CASSIOPEIA

WEST       FACING NORTH       EAST

NORTHERN
CIRCUMPOLAR CONSTELLATIONS
JULY 1 at 10 P.M.
JULY 16 at 9 P.M.
AUGUST 1 at 8 P.M.

## ACTIVITY: STAR DISK

### Purpose

To model the apparent daily movement of some northern circumpolar constellations.

### Materials

colored copy paper, such as bright green
Star Pattern
glue stick
8-by-8-inch (25-by-25-cm) –square piece of corrugated cardboard
scissors
box backboard (see Appendix 4)
fine-tip black marker
wide-tip black marker
pushpin
paper brad

### Procedure

1. Make a photocopy of Star Pattern, enlarged 140%, on the colored copy paper.

2. Cut out the star pattern circle and glue it to the cardboard.

3. Allow the glue to dry, then cut out the circle. The circle will be a star wheel.

4. Use the fine-tip marker to label the constellations and Polaris, as shown in the diagram.

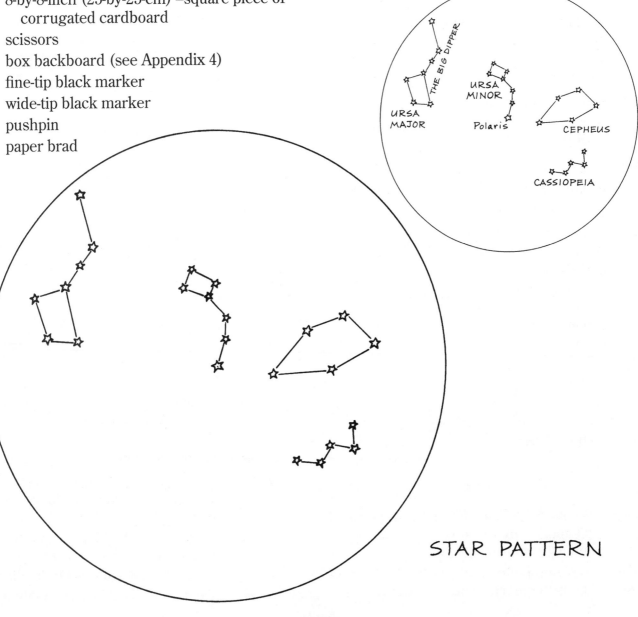

STAR PATTERN

5. Make a box backboard using the instructions in Appendix 4.

6. Use the wide-point marker to print a title, such as "Circumpolar Stars," on the top of the center panel of the backboard.

7. Use the pushpin to make a hole through the star Polaris on the star wheel.

8. With the pushpin through Polaris, hold the star wheel against the center panel of the backboard. Position the wheel so that it is centered on the panel beneath the title. Push the pin through the backboard. Hollow out the holes in the wheel and backboard with the pin so that it is large enough to insert the paper brad.

9. Insert the brad through the wheel and backboard. Open the brad on the back side of the backboard.

10. Use the wide-tip marker to print "Facing North," "East," and "West" on the backboard, as shown.

11. Demonstrate the apparent movement of the northern circumpolar stars on the wheel by turning the wheel in a counterclockwise direction.

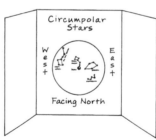

## Results

You have made a model of the movement of four northern circumpolar constellations.

## Why?

Polaris is called the Pole Star or North Star because it apparently remains in the same place in the sky: almost exactly above the North Pole, night after night. Face Polaris, and you will be facing north. Thus, to your right is east, to your left is west, and directly behind you is south.

Observe the northern sky for a period of time, and you will find that from night to night some stars appear to move in circular paths around Polaris. Like horses on a carousel, the stars appear to spin around a center point, but they still stay in line with one another. Thus, the shapes of constellations do not change even though they appear in different places during the night and on different nights of the year. From latitudes 40° N or greater, the four most visible northern circumpolar constellations are Ursa Major, Ursa Minor, Cassiopeia, and Cepheus. All stars, including the stars in these constellations, are most visible at their highest point in the sky.

## ON YOUR OWN!

1. Make models of each of the northern circumpolar constellations following these steps:

   a. Fold a sheet of black construction paper in half two times. One fold should be from top to bottom and the other from side to side.

   b. Use a compass to draw a 4-inch (10-cm) circle on the folded paper. Cut out the circle, cutting through all the layers of the folded paper.

   c. Make a photocopy of Star Pattern II on page 19, enlarged 140%, on white copy paper. Cut around each constellation, along the dashed line.

   d. Lay a 6-inch (15-cm) or larger square piece of thick corrugated cardboard on a table. The cardboard will protect the table. Place one of the black paper circles on the cardboard, then center one of the cut-out constellations on the black paper circle. Using a pushpin, punch a

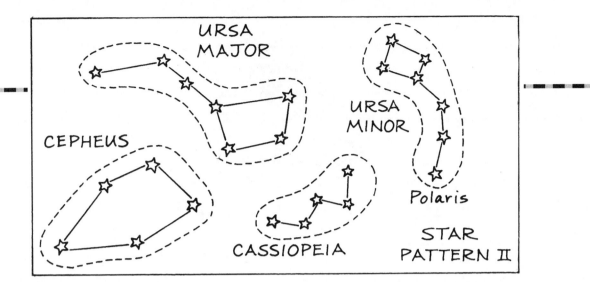

URSA
MAJOR

URSA
MINOR

CEPHEUS

Polaris

CASSIOPEIA

STAR
PATTERN II

hole through each star and also through the black paper. Remove the cut-out constellation. Using a paper hole punch, punch out small white circles from the white copy paper. With glue, stick one white cut-out circle over each star hole that you punched in the black paper.

**e.** Repeat the previous step for the other three constellations, making a model for each one.

**2.** Using glue, attach the constellation models to the side panels of your backboard.

**3.** Prepare and display an information sheet beneath each constellation model. Prepare the information sheet by folding a piece of copy paper, the same color as used for the star wheel, in half two times. First fold from top to bottom, then from side to side. Unfold the paper and cut along the folds, forming four equal-size pieces. Print the name of a different constellation on each sheet. Add information about each constellation, such as the following:

• **Ursa Major:** The name *Ursa Major* means "Great Bear." The entire constellation of Ursa Major may not always be the easiest to find, but the **asterism** (a group of stars with a shape within a constellation) in it is. Ursa Major's famous asterism is made of seven bright stars forming the shape of a large dipper. Hence the name: the Big Dipper.

• **Ursa Minor:** The name *Ursa Minor* means "Little Bear." This constellation is more commonly known as the Little Dipper. The upward bend in the dipper's handle forms the bear's tail, and the bowl is the bear's chest. The star at the end of the handle or bear's tail is Polaris.

• **Cassiopeia:** The Greeks imagined that the stars in Cassiopeia form a queen sitting on her throne, gazing at herself in a mirror. Cassiopeia is located on the opposite side of Polaris from the Big Dipper. The W shape of this constellation opens toward Polaris.

• **Cepheus:** Accompanying Cassiopeia in the sky is her husband, Cepheus, the King. The stars of this constellation are more difficult to find than the W shape of the queen's stars. The most obvious of Cepheus's stars are five that, when visually connected, form what looks like a simple drawing of a house. As with the queen, it takes a vivid imagination to picture the king sitting on his throne.

## BOOK LIST

Rey, Hans Augusto. *Find the Constellations.* New York: Houghton Mifflin, 1989. Describes stars and constellations throughout the year and offers ways of identifying them.

VanCleave, Janice. *Janice VanCleave's Constellations for Every Kid.* New York: Wiley, 1997. Fun, simple constellation experiments, including information about circumpolar stars and constellations.

———. *Janice VanCleave's Help! My Science Project Is Due Tomorrow!* Hoboken, N.J.: Wiley, 2001. Easy science projects, including ones about constellations that you can do overnight.

# Splat!

## *Make a Model of Impact Craters!*

**Meteoroids** are all the solid **debris** (scattered pieces of something that has been broken) in our solar system orbiting the Sun. If a meteoroid enters Earth's atmosphere, the meteoroid becomes very hot due to **friction** (a force that opposes the motion of two surfaces in contact with each other). The meteoroid **vaporizes** (changes to a gas), or burns up due to the friction with air in Earth's atmosphere. This produces light energy. When a meteoroid enters the atmosphere of a celestial body, it is then referred to as a **meteor**. Meteor is also the name for the streak of light produced when a meteoroid vaporizes as it passes through Earth's atmosphere. This light is commonly called a **shooting star.** If any part of the original meteoroid that entered the atmosphere reaches the surface of a celestial body, such as Earth, it is then called a **meteorite** (a meteor that hits the surface of Earth or any celestial body).

Meteorites made of material similar to that found in the rocks on Earth's surface are called **stony meteorites.** Most meteorites range in size from a dust speck to slightly larger than a pea. But some are much larger. A large meteorite hitting Earth or any celestial body produces an **impact crater** (a bowl-shaped depression caused by the impact of a solid body).

The most well preserved meteor crater on Earth is the Barringer Meteorite Crater in Arizona. This crater was formed about 50,000 years ago by a meteorite as large as a house. The Barringer Crater is about ¾ mile (1.2 km) in diameter and 667 feet (200 m) deep.

## ACTIVITY: IMPACTING

### Purpose

To make a model of an impact crater.

### Materials

5 cups (1,250 mL) plaster of Paris
shoe box–size plastic container
1-cup (250-mL) measuring cup
tap water
craft stick
lemon-size rock
petroleum jelly
timer
1 white sticky label, about 1-by-3 inches (2-by-7cm)
1 round toothpick
pen

### Procedure

1. Pour the plaster in the plastic container.

2. Add 2½ cups of water to the container of plaster.

3. Use the craft stick to mix the plaster and water.

4. Shake the container to smooth the surface of the plaster.

5. Allow the plaster to sit undisturbed for 20 minutes.

## HOW AN IMPACT CRATER IS MADE

First, the meteorite strikes the surface at several miles (km) per second, causing surface material to be ejected.

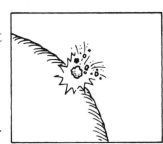

Second, the meteorite's energy of motion is transferred into shock waves and heat. The shock waves spread through the ground, **compressing** (pressing together) and **fracturing** (breaking with rough or jagged edges) it. The heat vaporizes most of the meteorite and some of the surface material.

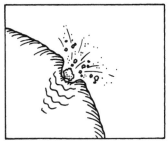

Third, the super-heated vapor causes an explosion at ground level that ejects material. The volume of material blown out is much larger than that of the meteorite, so even small objects can produce large holes. Because the explosion occurs belowground, even meteorites that strike at an angle produce a rounded hole.

Fourth, the ejected material falls back to the surface, partially filling the hole and forming a layer around the crater called an **ejecta blanket.**

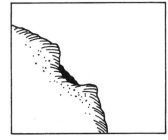

High-speed ejecta fall at greater distances from the crater, often digging small secondary craters where they strike the surface.

---

**6.** Cover the rock with a layer of petroleum jelly.

**7.** Set the box of plaster on the floor.

**8.** Stand next to the box and hold the rock waist high above the center of the plaster in the container. Drop the rock.

**9.** Carefully remove the rock from the plaster so that you disturb the plaster as little as possible.

**10.** Repeat steps 8 and 9 three or four times, dropping the rock on different parts of the plaster.

**11.** Prepare a flag label as shown, following these steps:

   **a.** Put just the ends of the sticky sides of the label together. Do not crease the fold.

   **b.** Carefully press the sticky sides of the label together, leaving a gap near the folded end.

   **c.** Insert one end of the toothpick through the gap and stick the toothpick to the folded end of the label. Press the label halves together around the toothpick.

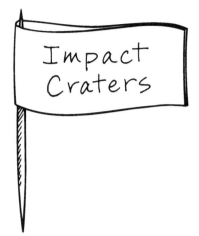

**d.** Use the pen to write "Impact Craters" on the flag.

**e.** Stick the flag in the plaster.

### Results

You have made a model of impact craters.

### Why?

*Crater* is from the Greek word meaning "cup" or "bowl." The surface of the Moon has many craters. Most are formed by impact cratering caused by meteorites slamming into the Moon's surface. The size of a crater is related to the energy of the meteorite forming it, which is determined by the size and mass of the object and its speed. The impact of the meteorite was demonstrated in making the crater model. But unlike real crater formation, there was no explosion to make the hole larger than the meteorite hitting the surface or fall-back of ejecta material.

### ON YOUR OWN!

The impact crater model can be displayed in front of a box backboard. To make a box backboard, see Appendix 4. Attach a flap book (see Appendix 5) to the box backboard to provide information about the four steps of impact crater formation described on page 21 of this book. Use two different colored pieces of poster board to make the flap book. For example, if the box is covered in white paper, the small poster board square could be white and the larger framing square could be red or any bright color. Diagrams of the steps of impact crater formation can be drawn in the space beneath each flap along with information about the steps.

### BOOK LIST

Koppeschar, Carl. *Moon Handbook.* Chico, Calif.: Moon Publications, 1995. Information about the Moon, including its craters and how they were formed.

VanCleave, Janice. *Janice VanCleave's Help! My Science Project Is Due Tomorrow!* Hoboken, N.J.: Wiley, 2001. Easy science projects, including ones about impact craters, that you can do overnight.

# II

# BIOLOGY

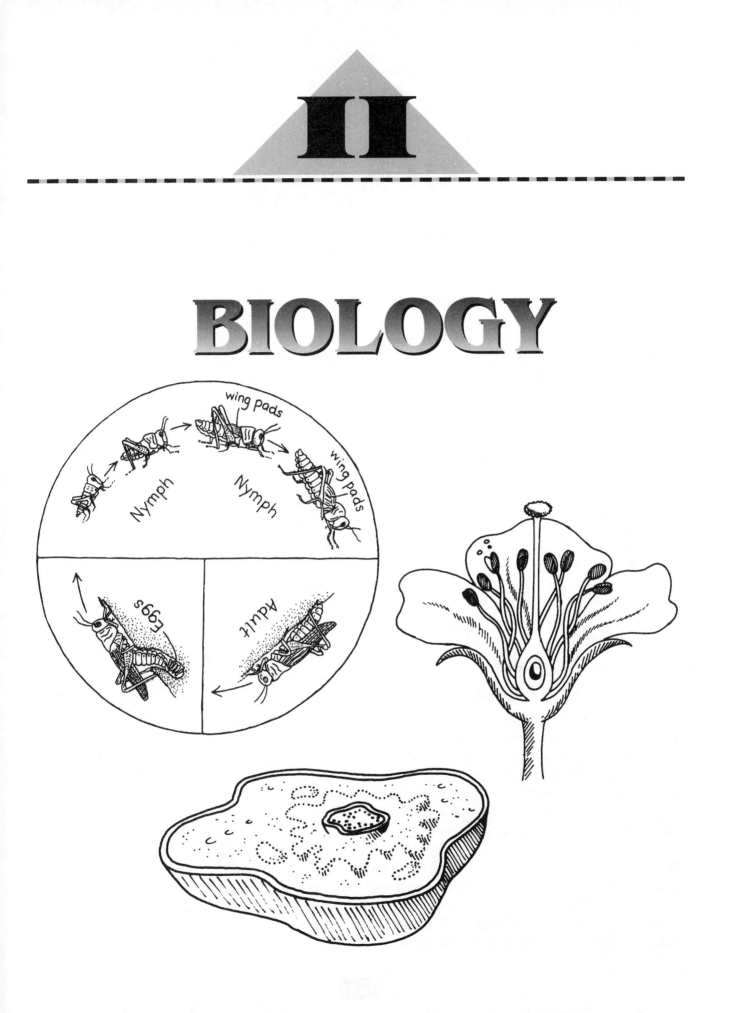

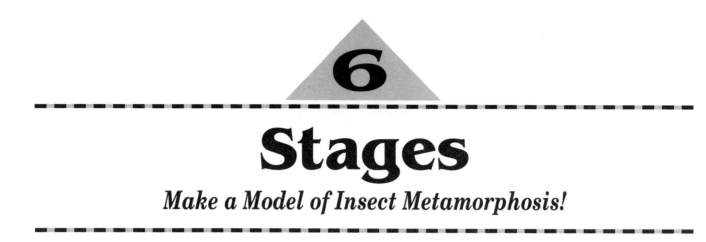

# Stages

## *Make a Model of Insect Metamorphosis!*

Insects develop in several distinct stages. An insect life cycle that consists of four stages, from egg to larva to pupa to adult, is called **complete metamorphosis.** Ants, beetles, fleas, flies, ladybugs, and butterflies are among the insects that develop by complete metamorphosis.

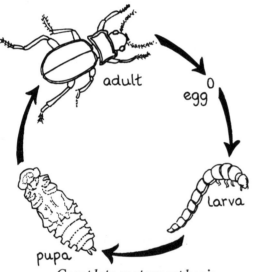

*Complete metamorphosis*

In complete metamorphosis, after mating, the adult female insect lays **eggs** (first stage of metamorphosis), which develop into **larvae** (the wormlike active second stage). The larvae of moths and butterflies are called caterpillars; those of some flies are called maggots. Larvae eat large amounts of food and generally grow quickly. As they grow they periodically molt. **Molting** is a process of shedding the **exoskeleton,** which is their outer covering. Larvae molt many times before reaching the pupa stage. A **pupa** is the immobile third and resting stage of complete metamorphosis. **Chrysalis** is the

name of the hard-shelled pupa stage of certain insects, especially butterflies. **Cocoon** is the name of the protective silk covering for the pupa stage of many insects, especially moths. The cocoon is spun by the larva. During the pupa stage the wormlike larva changes into an adult. When all the changes have occurred, the adult pushes and breaks open the outer covering surrounding it and gets out. The adult looks for food and searches for a mate. After mating, the females lay eggs and the cycle starts over again.

Some insects, such as grasshoppers, develop in only three stages from egg to nymph to adult; there is no larva or pupa stage. This type of insect development is called **incomplete metamorphosis.** The **nymph** is the young insect, which looks like the adult, but is smaller and wingless. Nymphs grow through a series of molts. As nymphs of winged

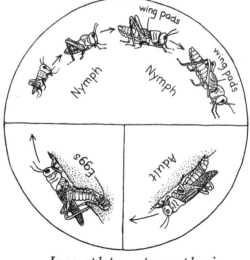

*Incomplete metamorphosis*

insects grow, small winglike growths called wing pads appear. The **wing pads** increase in size only slightly up to the last molt. After the last molt, the adult appears with wings expanded to their full size.

## ACTIVITY: BUTTERFLY METAMORPHOSIS

### Purpose

To model butterfly metamorphosis.

### Materials

five 6-by-9-inch (15-by-22.5-cm) unlined index cards
pencil
ruler
scissors
glue stick
photocopy of page 26, "Stages of Butterfly Metamorphosis"

### Procedure

**1.** Make the pages of a pop-up book by following these steps:

**a.** Fold one of the index cards in half by placing the short ends together.

**b.** In the center of the fold, draw a 1-inch (2.5-cm) square.

**c.** Cut down lines A and B to make a pop-up stand.

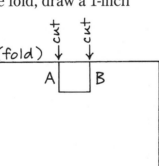

**d.** Bend the pop-up stand forward and crease it along line C. Bend it backward and again crease along line C.

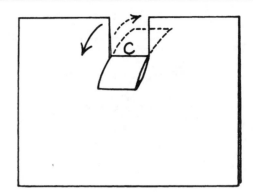

**e.** Unfold the card.

**f.** Using your fingers, pull the cut pop-up stand toward the inside of the card.

**g.** Close the card and press the surface of the card to crease the folds on the card and the pop-up stand inside the card.

**h.** Repeat each of the previous steps, using the remaining four cards.

**2.** Cut out figures A through F from the photocopied butterfly metamorphosis stages page by cutting around each figure.

**3.** Prepare the first two pages of the book by unfolding one of the cards. Number the pages by writing "1" in the upper right corner of one of the short sides of the card and "2" in the lower right corner. Label the top of page 1 above the pop-up stand "Butterfly

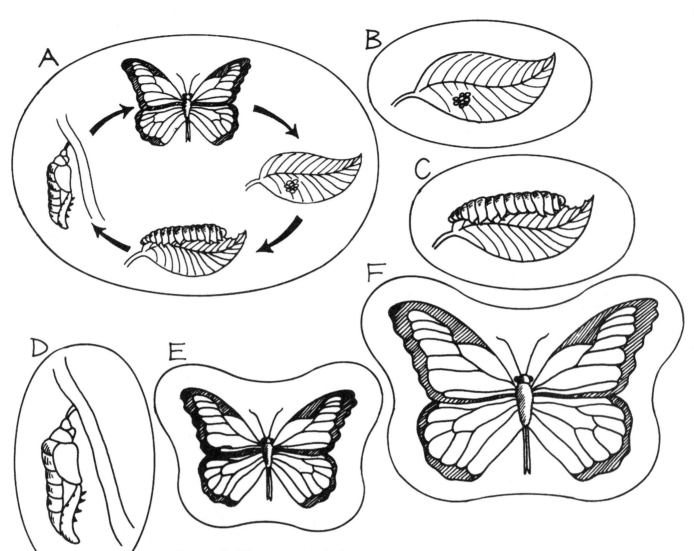

*Butterfly Metamorphosis Stages*

Metamorphosis," as shown. Note that the pages will lift from bottom to top instead of from right to left. Be sure the bottom edge of Fig. A sits even with the bottom of the pop-up stand.

**4.** With the card partially opened, use the glue stick to place glue on the front side of the pop-up stand. Stick Figure A on the glue.

**5.** Repeat steps 3 and 4 four times using Figures B through E. Label the cards as follows: pages 3 and 4, "Stage 1, Eggs" (Figure B); pages 5 and 6, "Stage 2, Caterpillar" (Figure C);

pages 7 and 8, "Stage 3, Chrysalis" (Figure D); pages 9 and 10, "Stage 4, Adult" (Figure E).

**6.** Glue the backs of these pages together: 2 and 3, 4 and 5, 6 and 7, 8 and 9. Allow the glue to dry.

**7.** Close the book and press it with your fingers to flatten it as much as possible.

**8.** Glue Figure F to the front cover of the book and add the title "Butterfly Metamorphosis."

## Results

You have made a model of the steps of the complete metamorphosis of a butterfly.

## Why?

The adult female butterfly of most species usually lays eggs on a plant. The eggs develop into larvae, commonly called caterpillars. The plant the eggs are laid on cannot be just any plant, but must be a plant that the caterpillar can eat. Like all larvae, butterfly caterpillars eat, grow, molt, and eat some more. When they are ready to pupate, most stop eating and move more slowly. Many change colors before pupating. They look for a suitable place to secure themselves with a silk thread made in their body. The larva molts, then a liquid covering the body hardens. The hard-shelled pupa formed by a butterfly is called a chrysalis.

When the adult butterfly breaks out of its chrysalis, it generally hangs from the broken chrysalis or nearby twig until it is ready to fly. The butterfly holds out its wings and flaps them slowly. This pumps blood into the wings, causing them to expand. The wings quickly harden into this expanded shape. The butterfly is ready to fly and find food. Butterflies feed on a variety of materials, including rotting food, but most seek out flowers from which they drink **nectar** (a sugary liquid produced in many flowers at the base of their petals, which is food for many insects).

## ON YOUR OWN!

**1.** The pop-up book shows the four stages of complete metamorphosis of a butterfly. Add information to each page of the book, starting with page 2, where the pop-up picture is of the complete metamorphosis cycle. You may wish to define complete metamorphosis on this page and give general information about the cycle. Then continue providing information about each stage represented by each of the pop-up pictures. You may color the figures.

**2.** Make a pop-up book representing the incomplete metamorphosis of an insect, such as a grasshopper. Use the original instructions for creating the pop-up book, but draw your own pictures to show the stages of incomplete metamorphosis, or make an enlarged copy of the picture showing incomplete metamorphosis in the introduction to this chapter.

**3.** You can make a larger pop-up book using larger pieces of poster board for the pages. Both types of metamorphosis, complete and incomplete, could be represented at the same time by showing each stage side by side on the pages. You would need to make two pop-up stands per card to show the shapes side by side.

## BOOK LIST

Pringle, Laurence. *An Extraordinary Life.* New York: Orchard Books, 1997. Introduces the life cycle, feeding habits, migration patterns, and mating habits of the monarch butterfly through observation of one particular monarch that the author named Danaus.

VanCleave, Janice. *Janice VanCleave's Insects and Spiders.* New York: Wiley, 1998. Experiments about metamorphosis and other insect topics. Each chapter contains ideas that can be turned into award-winning science fair projects.

Wright, Amy Bartlett. *Peterson First Guides: Caterpillars.* New York: Houghton Mifflin, 1993. Information about insect metamorphosis, how to raise caterpillars to adults, and 120 of the most common caterpillars in North America.

# 7

# Building Blocks
*Make a Model of a Cell!*

A **cell** is the smallest structure that is able to perform basic life processes, such as taking in nutrients, giving off waste, and reproducing. Cells are the building blocks of all **organisms** (living things). Some organisms are **unicellular** (made of one cell), but most organisms are multicellular (made of many cells). In a **multicellular** organism, each cell has a special function that benefits the other cells. The different cells all depend on each other.

There are two basic types of cells: **prokaryotic** cells, without a nucleus, and **eukaryotic cells,** with a nucleus. A **nucleus** is a spherical or oval-shaped body in a cell that controls cell activity. Prokaryotic cells are found only in **bacteria** (unicellular organisms made of prokaryotic cells) and **cyanobacteria** (formerly called blue-green algae), which are unicellular organisms. All other organisms, including plants and animals, are made of eukaryotic cells.

Eukaryotic cells have three basic cell parts. First, the **cell membrane** is the thin outer skin that holds a cell together, protects the inner parts, and allows materials to move into and out of the cell. Second, the **cytoplasm** is a clear, jellylike material made mostly of water,

occupying the region between the nucleus and the cell membrane, containing substances and particles that work together to sustain life. Third is the nucleus.

The specialized cells of multicellular organisms are organized into five basic levels: cells, tissues, organs, organ systems, and organism. The cell itself is at the first level of organization. For example, in animals there are many types of cells, such as blood cells and muscle cells. Groups of similar cells with similar functions form the second level of organization, called **tissue.** Similar muscle cells form **muscle tissue,** which is responsible for movement. **Blood** in **vertebrates** (animals with a backbone) is considered a tissue made up of several types of blood cells suspended in a liquid called **plasma.** Blood transports oxygen and nutrients to cells and throughout the body and carries wastes away from cells.

An **organ** is a group of different tissues working together to perform a special job, and is the third level of organization. The heart is an organ made up of different types of tissue, including blood tissue and muscle tissue. **Blood vessels** are tubelike organs made of layers of different tissue through which blood flows.

The fourth level is an **organ system,** which is a group of organs working together to perform a special job. In animals, there are many different organ systems. One example, the **circulatory system** (body parts that work together to transport blood throughout the body) is made up of organs, including the heart

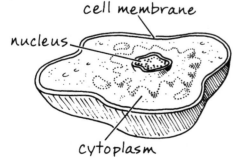

cell membrane

nucleus

cytoplasm

and blood vessels. Another example, the **respiratory system** (body parts that work together to help you breathe), is made up of organs, including the **nose** (the organ where air enters the body), **bronchi** (short tubes that direct air into the lungs), and **lungs** (organs where gas is exchanged). When all the systems work together, they form an organism.

An organism is the highest level of cellular organization. A single living organism is the combination of all its systems, which are made up of organs made up of tissues made up of cells made up of cell parts.

In 1665, the English scientist Robert Hooke (1635–1703) was one of the first to see cells. Hooke observed thin slices of bark (cork) with a simple microscope of his own making. He thought the rows of tiny, empty boxes looked like rooms in a monastery, which were called cells. So he named the small plant units cells. The Dutch microscope maker Antonie van Leeuwenhoek (1632–1723) was the first to see and describe bacteria, the smallest of all cells. As microscopes improved, scientists discovered that all organisms were made of cells.

The size of multicellular organisms is determined by the number of their cells and not the size of their cells. Cells vary in size, with the smallest being bacteria cells. Some bacteria have a diameter of about 0.000004 inches (0.00001 cm). It would take 10,000 of these bacteria in a row to be about as wide as the diameter of a human hair. Among the largest cells are the nerve cells in a giraffe's neck. These cells can be more than 9.7 ft (3 m) in length. About 10,000 average size human cells can fit on the head of a pin, and it is estimated that the human body contains from 20 trillion to 30 trillion cells.

## ACTIVITY: BASIC CELL MODEL
## Purpose

To make a basic cell model for an animal or a plant.

## Materials

4 white sticky labels, about 1-by-3-inches (2.5-by-7.5-cm)
2 toothpicks
fine-point black permanent marker
crayon, your choice of color
½-inch (1.25-cm) Styrofoam ball
empty 2-liter plastic soda bottle
2 cups (500 mL) plaster of Paris
1 cup (250 mL) measuring cup
tap water
craft stick
paper towels
adult helper

## Procedure

1. Fold one label in half, touching the ends together but leaving the fold open. Place a toothpick in the fold. Press the label halves together around the toothpick.

2. Use the marker to write "Nucleus" on each side of the folded-over label.

3. Using a second label, repeat steps 1 and 2, writing "Cytoplasm" on each side of the label.

4. Ask an adult to cut the Styrofoam ball in half. Color both halves, including the cut surface, with the crayon.

5. Ask an adult to cut the bottom 3 inches (7.5 cm) from the soda bottle. Discard the top part.

6. Pour the plaster of Paris into the bottom section of the soda bottle.

7. Slowly add ½ cup (125 mL) of water to the plaster, stirring as you add the water. The

mixture should be thick, but thin enough to move so the surface is smooth if the container is shaken. If it is too thin, add a small amount of plaster. If it is too thick, add a small amount of water.
*CAUTION: Discard the stick in the trash. Do not get plaster in the sink because it can clog the drain.*

**8.** Use the paper towels to clean the outside of the container as well as the inside above the surface of the plaster. Discard the paper towels.

**9.** Push about half of the rounded side of one of the colored halves of the Styrofoam ball into the center of the wet plaster. Keep the remaining half of the ball for the next activity.

**10.** Stand the toothpick with the "Cytoplasm" label in the plaster.

**11.** Stick the toothpick with the "Nucleus" label in the Styrofoam ball.

**12.** Use the marker to write "Cell Membrane" on one of the remaining labels. Place the label inside the container and just above the plaster, as shown.

**13.** Write "Basic Cell Parts" on the fourth label and place it on the outside of the container.

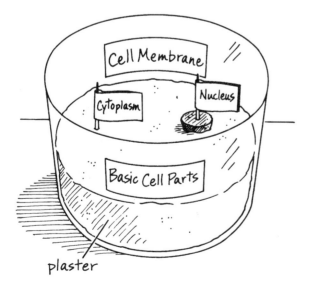

plaster

**14.** Allow the plaster to dry, which will take about 20 to 30 minutes.

## Result

You have made a model that represents half of a cell with the three basic cell parts.

## Why?

Cells may differ in size and shape, but cells of plants and animals have three basic parts: cell membrane, cytoplasm, and nucleus. In your model, the cell membrane is represented by the container, the cytoplasm is represented by the plaster, and the nucleus is represented by the Styrofoam ball. While the parts of your cell model are rigid, the parts of real cells are soft and pliable (bendable).

## ON YOUR OWN!

Although there are differences in animal cells, all animal cells contain the three basic parts: cell membrane, cytoplasm, and nucleus. They also can include other parts, such as mitochondria and ribosomes. Design an animal cell model with more parts listed. One way is to use a larger container, such as a plastic tray or large resealable bag. You can use things like marbles, peanut shells, and ribbon to represent different cell parts. The parts can be numbered as well as labeled, and a legend can be created using a layered book. (See Appendix 2 for instructions on making a layered book.) The pages of the book will match the identifying numbers on the cell model, and information about each cell part can be included in the layered book. In the example shown in the illustration on page 31, there are eight cell parts. The following descriptions would be given in the layered book.

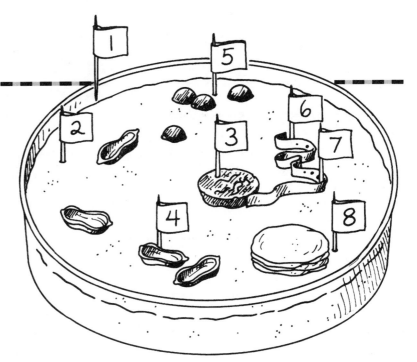

1. **Cell membrane:** The outer boundary of the cell, which holds the cell together and protects the inner parts.

2. **Cytoplasm:** A clear, jellylike material made mostly of water, occupying the region between the nucleus and the cell membrane and containing **organelles,** which are small organs that work together to sustain life.

3. **Nucleus:** A spherical or oval-shaped body in a cell that houses the things that control cell activity.

4. **Mitochondria:** The cells' power stations, where food and oxygen react to produce the energy needed for the cells to work and live.

5. **Lysosomes:** Sacs found in cells that contain chemicals used to destroy harmful substances or worn-out cell parts. Numerous in disease-fighting cells, such as white blood cells, that destroy harmful invaders or cell debris.

6. **Endoplasmic reticulum (ER):** A network of tubes that manufacture, process, and transport materials within cells containing a nucleus. The ER connects to the nuclear membrane and extends into the cytoplasm. There are two types of ER: rough and smooth. Rough ER is covered with ribosomes.

7. **Ribosomes:** Tiny structures found free in the cytoplasm or on the surface of the endoplasmic reticulum. The structure where **protein** (nutrient used for growth and repair) is made.

8. **Golgi bodies:** The structure where proteins are stored until needed. Has the appearance of flattened sacs, much like stacks of pita bread or cotton pads.

| Cell Parts | |
|---|---|
| Cell Membrane | 1 |
| Cytoplasm | 2 |
| Nucleus | 3 |
| Mitochondria | 4 |
| Lysosomes | 5 |
| Endoplasmic Reticulum | 6 |
| Ribosomes | 7 |
| Golgi Bodies | 8 |

## BOOK LIST

Bender, Lionel. *Human Body.* New York: Crescent Books, 1992. The inside story of the human body, from cells, the building blocks of life, to complex systems.

Ganeri, Anita. *The Usborne Book of Body Facts.* London: Usborne, 1992. Hundreds of facts and figures about the human body, including the cell.

Hoagland, Mahlon, and Bert Dodson. *The Way Life Works.* New York: Random House, 1998. Information and simple colored art explain how all organisms function in astonishingly similar, yet amazing ways. Facts about the basic building blocks of organisms, cells, are included.

Meredith, Susan, Ann Goldman, and Tom Lissauer. *The Usborne Young Scientist Human Body.* London: Usborne, 1992. Exciting scientific topics, including cells, are explained in a clear visual style.

VanCleave, Janice. *Janice VanCleave's The Human Body for Every Kid.* New York: Wiley, 1995. Fun, simple human body experiments, including information about cells.

# Movers

## *Make a Model of Muscles!*

Your body is like a marionette, which is a puppet with strings attached to different parts. As the strings are pulled, the puppet's parts move. Instead of having strings attached to your body you have muscle tissue, which is tissue found in animals that causes the animal to move. When muscles **contract** (shorten) and **relax** (lengthen) motion occurs. Muscles attached to bones pull on the bones, making them move, much as the strings move the parts of the marionette. Without muscles you could not move.

Muscles are the only type of body tissue that have the ability to contract and relax. Not all muscles are attached to bone; some form organs, such as blood vessels, the heart, and lungs. There are three types of muscles: skeletal muscles, cardiac muscles, and smooth muscles. **Skeletal muscles** are attached to your bones and move your body. Since you have control over your body's motion, skeletal muscles are called **voluntary muscles** (muscles that can be controlled at will). The two remaining types of muscles, cardiac and smooth, are **involuntary muscles** (muscles that cannot be controlled at will). **Cardiac muscles** are found only in the heart and are made up of tightly woven cells. **Smooth muscles** are made up of cells that are long, thin, and pointed at the ends, and have one nucleus. These muscles are joined to form sheets of muscle tissue found in internal organs, such as the lungs and the stomach. They are also attached to hair. When you are cold, the smooth muscles attached to your body hairs contract, pulling up the hairs. The contracted

muscle creates a small bump on the skin around each hair, commonly called a **goose bump.** The cold can also cause your muscles to **shiver** or shake. The muscle movements that cause shivering, goose bumps, and heartbeats happen without your thinking about them, which is why they are called involuntary.

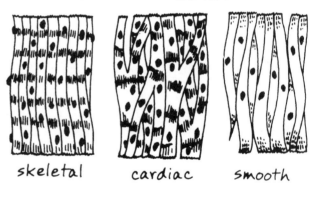

MUSCLE TISSUE

skeletal     cardiac     smooth

The work done by muscles during contracting and relaxing also produces much of the heat that keeps your body warm.

### ACTIVITY: LIFTER

#### Purpose

To make a model of how skeletal muscles move your arm.

## Materials

two 3-by-8-inch (7.5-by-20-cm) pieces
   of poster board
paper hole punch
1 paper brad
pencil
one 14-inch (35-cm) and one
   18-inch (45-cm) piece of thick
   string

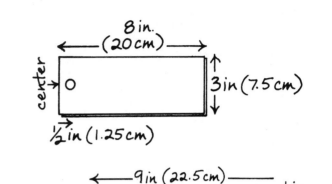

## Procedure

1. Place the poster board strips
   together. Use the paper hole
   punch to cut a hole through both
   strips about ½ inch (1.25 cm)
   from the center point on one end.

2. Connect the strips by putting the
   paper brad through the holes in
   both strips and bending back the metal to
   hold the pieces together.

3. Swivel one of the strips around the brad so
   that the strips are in a straight line, and label
   the upper arm and forearm, as shown. This
   is your arm model.

4. Use the paper hole punch to cut two holes
   near the top edge of the arm, one 1 inch (2.5
   cm) and the other 9 inches (22.5 cm) from
   the right end of the arm.

5. Repeat step 4, cutting two holes near the
   bottom edge of the arm model.

6. Tie the ends of the shorter string, called
   string A, to the holes on the top edge of the
   arm model.

7. Tie the ends of the longer string, called
   string B, to the holes on the bottom edge of
   the arm model.

8. Lay the arm model on a table. Holding the
   upper arm against the table, pull string A
   away from the arm. Note the motion of the
   forearm.

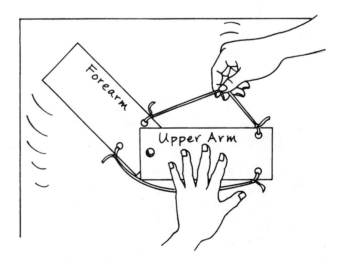

9. Release string A and pull string B away from
   the arm. Note the motion of the forearm.

## Results

You have made a model of an arm. Pulling on string A moves the forearm of the model so that the arm bends at the brad. Pulling on string B moves the forearm back to its original position.

## Why?

Muscles can pull but not push, so skeletal muscles work in pairs to create movement. The arm model shows how a pair of muscles bends and straightens the arm. Muscles that bend **joints** (places where two bones meet) are called **flexors,** and muscles that straighten joints are called **extensors.** In the arm model, string A represents the **biceps** muscle, which is the large flexor muscle on the front side of your upper arm. The biceps muscle moves the **forearm** (the part of the arm between the elbow and the wrist) so that the arm bends at the **elbow.** The elbow is the joint that connects the bones of your upper and lower arm and the **wrist** is the joint between the forearm and the hand. (See Chapter 9 for more about joints.) String B represents the extensor muscle on the back of the upper arm called the **triceps** muscle. These two muscles control the bending of your arm at the elbow.

## ON YOUR OWN!

Some skeletal muscles are attached directly to bones, while others are attached to bones by **tendons** (tough, nonelastic tissues that attach some skeletal muscles to bones). Design a way to identify the muscles and tendons in the arm model. One way is to color-code the string. Using a red marker, color the strings red except for about 1 inch (2.5 cm) at each end. The red section represents the muscle, and the white ends represent the tendons. You can use tags to label the biceps muscle "A" and the triceps muscle "B" as shown. You could cut out a hand shape from poster board and tape it to the end of the forearm. A legend could be written on the hand that identifies the parts of the model: muscle, tendon, biceps, and triceps.

## BOOK LIST

Allison, Linda. *Blood and Guts.* Boston: Little, Brown & Company, 1976. Facts and activities about the human body, including muscles.

VanCleave, Janice. *Janice VanCleave's The Human Body for Every Kid.* New York: Wiley, 1995. Fun, simple human body experiments, including information about muscles.

Weiner, Esther. *The Incredible Human Body.* New York: Scholastic, 1996. Information about the human body, including how muscles move an arm.

Wyse, Liz. *Make It Work! Body.* Ocala, Fla.: Action Publishing, 1994. Human body models, including an arm.

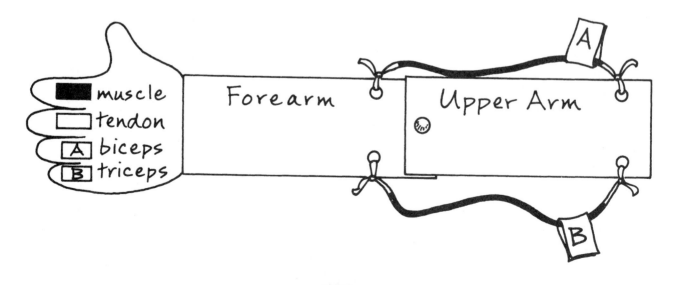

# Jointed

## Make a Model of Joints!

Before birth, a human baby's skeleton is made of **cartilage** (a firm but flexible tissue that gives shape and support to the bodies of some animals). But by birth, most of that cartilage has changed into about 350 bones. As the baby grows, many of these bones grow together. An adult skeleton has about 206 bones. Cartilage still makes up some parts of the adult skeleton.

Where bones come together is called a joint. Some are **fixed joints** (joints that allow no movement), such as the bones of the skull and teeth in their sockets. Other joints are **slightly movable joints** (joints that have limited motion). Your ribs are attached to your **spine** (backbone) by slightly movable joints. The joints in the middle of your feet and the palms of your hands are also only slightly movable. Most joints, however, are **movable joints** (joints that are able to move freely). These joints are held together by **connective tissue** (tissue that holds internal body parts, including bones, together) called ligaments. A **ligament** is a tough band of slightly elastic connective tissue.

There are different types of movable joints that allow for different types of movement. The most mobile type is the **ball-and-socket joint,** such as the joint between your thigh and hip bones. The end of the thigh bone is round like a ball and fits into a cup-shaped socket in the hip bone. This type of joint allows

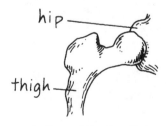

*Ball-and-Socket Joint*

you to raise and lower your leg as well as to turn it. Where your upper arm meets the shoulder is another example of a ball-and-socket joint.

A **hinge joint,** such as those of the knees, elbows, and fingers, does not rotate. Instead, the bones of this joint can move in only one

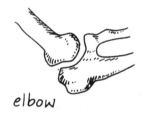

*Hinge Joint*

direction, like the hinge on a door. In the elbow, the rounded end of the humerus bone of the upper arm fits into a cradle formed by the ulna and radius bones of the forearm. The elbow allows the bones of the lower arm to be raised and lowered.

The skull can **pivot** (rotate) because of a **pivot joint** (a joint that allows rotation). In this joint the **vertebra** (one of the bony structures that make up the spine)

*Pivot Joint*

at the top of the spine fits over a peg on the vertebra below it, allowing the head to move from side to side.

Vertebrae in your spine and the bones in your wrist are linked by **gliding joints** (joints in which the bones easily move over one another). The bones in these joints fit together like smooth puzzle pieces.

Some bones are connected by different joints. These joints together are called **compound joints** (several joints between bones

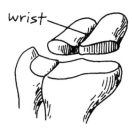

*Gliding Joint*

that work together to allow the bones to move in different directions). For example, your forearm can rotate because the two bones of your forearm (the ulna and radius) are connected by a pivot joint. These bones also connect to the humerus bone of the upper arm by a hinge joint, allowing the forearm to be raised. The compound joints in your neck allow your head to move in different directions, including from side to side, nodding up and down, as well as in a circular motion.

Movable joints need a **lubricant** (a substance that reduces friction between materials in contact with each other) and **cushioning** (soft padding material) that prevents the bones from grinding against each other. The ends of the bones in these joints are covered with cartilage, which acts as a cushion between the bones. These joints also contain a special fluid called **synovial fluid,** which is a lubricant.

## ACTIVITY: MOVABLE

### Purpose

To make a ball-and-socket joint model.

### Material

2-quart (2-L) bowl
1 pound (454 g) instant papier-mâché (air-dry clay also works well)
2-cup (500-mL) measuring cup
tap water
1-gallon (4-L) resealable plastic bag
craft stick
waxed paper

## Procedure

1. In the bowl, mix papier-mâché and water as indicated on the package.

2. Separate an apple-size piece of papier-mâché and place the remaining papier-mâché in the resealable bag. Store the bag in a refrigerator until needed.

3. Break the apple-size piece of papier-mâché in half. Form one of the pieces into a bowl shape. Set the bowl on a piece of waxed paper.

4. Shape the remaining piece of papier-mâché into a ball.

5. Stick about 1 inch (2.5 cm) of the craft stick into the ball. Squeeze the papier-mâché around the stick to secure it.

6. Cover the end of the ball with waxed paper. Then stand the waxed paper–covered ball inside the papier-mâché bowl. Reshape the bowl so that the sides of the bowl cover most of the ball.

7. With the ball inside the bowl, allow the bowl and ball to sit undisturbed overnight. They will be partially dry in the morning.

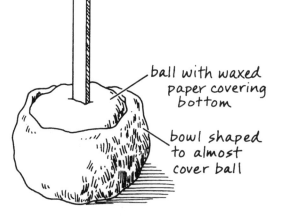

ball with waxed paper covering bottom

bowl shaped to almost cover ball

8. Touching the ball and not the stick, carefully rotate the ball to slightly enlarge the size of the bowl so that the ball has room to move and be removed from the bowl.

9. Allow the bowl and ball to sit undisturbed until they dry. This could take two or more days.

10. When the papier-mâché pieces are dry, remove the waxed paper, then hold the stick and move the ball around inside the bowl.

## Results

You have made a model of a ball-and-socket joint.

## Why?

In a ball-and-socket joint, one bone is movable and the other is fixed. The movable bone has a rounded end, represented by the ball-shaped papier-mâché model. This rounded end fits into a socket in a fixed bone, represented by the bowl-shaped papier-mâché model. The bone with the rounded end can move in all directions, including rotating around. In the shoulder joint, the rounded end of the humerus bone of the upper arm fits into a bowl-shaped socket in the **scapula** (shoulder bone). You can rotate your arm in a 360° vertical circle.

## ON YOUR OWN

1. Use papier-mâché to make models of a hinge joint, a pivot joint, and a gliding joint like the ones shown here.

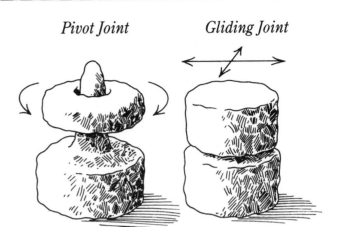

*Pivot Joint*  *Gliding Joint*

2. Design a way to display your models. One way is to stand the joint models in front of a three-paneled backboard. (See Appendix 1 for instructions on making the backboard.) Information sheets about each model can be glued to the backboard behind each model. Try these ideas for making the attached papers more visible:

- Use contrasting colors, such as white paper and a colored backboard.

- Mat the papers on colored material. See Appendix 6 for instructions on matting.

## BOOK LIST

Ganeri, Anita. *The Usborne Book of Body Facts.* London: Usborne, 1992. Hundreds of facts and figures about the human body, including joints.

Meredith, Susan, Ann Goldman, and Tom Lissauer. *The Usborne Young Scientist Human Body.* London: Usborne, 1992. Exciting scientific topics, including joints, explained in a clear visual style.

Parker, Steve. *The Skeleton and Movement.* New York: Franklin Watts, 1989. Detailed artwork including color photographs make it easy to learn about the human body's skeletal system.

VanCleave, Janice. *Janice VanCleave's The Human Body for Every Kid.* New York: Wiley, 1995. Fun, simple human body experiments, including information about the skeleton and joints.

*Hinge Joint*

# Seed Makers

*Make a Model of Flower Parts!*

**Angiosperms** are flowering plants. The **flower** is the reproductive system of these plants. A **reproductive system** contains organs for **reproduction** (the process by which new organisms are produced). The main job of a flower is to make **seeds** (the part of a flowering plant from which a new plant grows). Angiosperms reproduce by **sexual reproduction** (the forming of a new organism by fertilization). **Fertilization** is the union of **sperm** (a male reproductive cell) and an **egg** (a female reproductive cell). In plants, fertilization results in the formation of a seed.

The male reproductive organ of a flower is called the **stamen,** and the female reproductive organ is called the **carpel** or **pistil.** The stalklike portion of a stamen is called the **filament,** which supports the **anther.** The anther produces **pollen grains,** which produce sperm.

The carpel has three basic parts: the stigma, the style, and the ovary. The **stigma** is the sticky top that holds pollen grains that land on it. The **style** is a tubelike structure that supports the stigma and connects it with the rounded base of the carpel, called the **ovary** (the part of the carpel where seeds are formed).

Inside the ovary are seedlike parts called **ovules,** which contain eggs. The ovules ripen into seeds as a result of fertilization of the eggs by sperm. **Pollination** is the transfer of pollen grains from the anther to the stigma.

After pollination, the pollen grains begin to grow a long tube, called a **pollen tube,** down the style toward the eggs. Sperm move through pollen tubes to the eggs. After fertilization, the sepals, petals, and stamens wither and the ovary and the ovules develop. The ovary develops into a fruit and the ovules develop into the seeds inside the fruit.

Other flower parts not directly involved in making seeds include sepals and petals. **Sepals** are leaflike structures that surround and protect a flower before it opens. **Petals** are leaflike structures that surround and help protect a flower's reproductive organs. The colors and markings of petals attract insects and other animals that help with pollination. Color can attract insects from a distance, and once insects are close, the scent of the flower may further attract the insect. Between the base of the flower and the end of the **pedicel** (the stem that connects a flower to the rest of the plant) is the **receptacle,** which supports the flower.

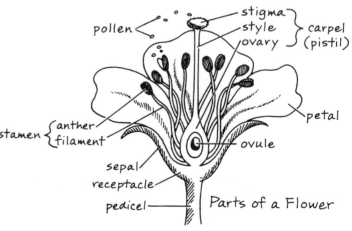

Parts of a Flower

## ACTIVITY: COMPLETE

### Purpose

To make a model of the parts of a flower.

### Materials

ruler

pencil

2 sheets of 9-by-12-inch (22.5-by-30-cm) construction paper—1 green, 1 red

scissors

glue

flexible drinking straw (use a green one if available)

4 tablespoons (60 mL) plaster of Paris

1 teaspoon (5 mL) measuring spoon

3-ounce (90-mL) paper cup

tap water

craft stick

paper towel

copy of "Flower Patterns" below

6-inch (15-cm) green pipe cleaner

paper hole punch

two 12-inch (30-cm) yellow pipe cleaners

6-by-10-inch (15-by-25-cm) piece of white poster board

pen

2 crayons—1 red, 1 green

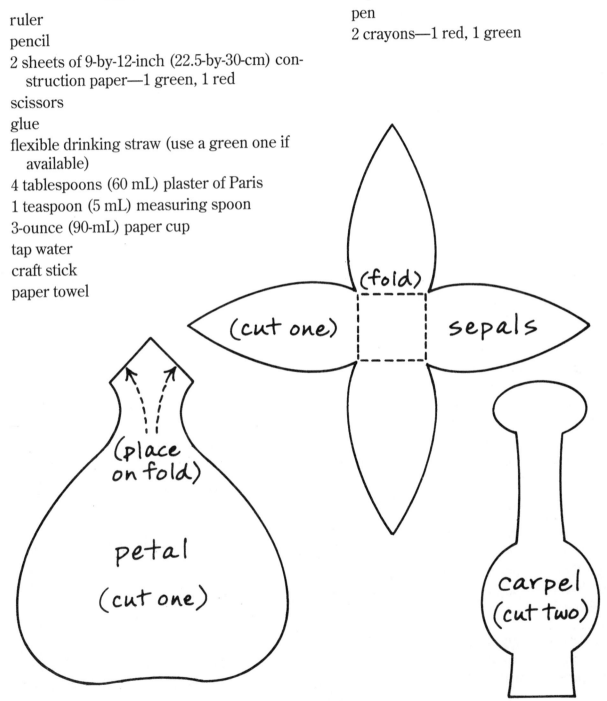

# Procedure

**1.** Use the ruler and pencil to mark a line across and ½ inch (1.25 cm) from one of the short ends of the green construction paper. Cut off the strip.

**2.** Cover one side of the green paper strip with glue, then wrap it around the flexible end of the straw so that it is about ¼ inch (0.63 cm) from the end of the straw. The wrapped strip represents a receptacle.

**3.** Put 4 tablespoons (60 mL) of plaster of Paris in the cup.

**4.** Add 4 teaspoons (20 mL) of water to the cup. Stir with the craft stick. *CAUTION: Discard the stick in the trash. Do not get plaster in the sink, because it can clog the drain.*

**5.** Use the paper towel to clean the outside of the cup as well as the inside of the cup above the surface of the plaster. Discard the paper towel.

**6.** Stand the straw in the center of the cup of plaster with the straw's flexible end up. Reposition the straw as needed until the plaster is firm enough to support the straw in a vertical position, which will be about 10 minutes.

**7.** Cut out the flower patterns.

**8.** Lay the sepal pattern on the piece of green construction paper. Draw around the pattern, then cut along the lines you drew.

**9.** Fold the remaining part of the green construction paper in half. Place the carpel pattern on the folded paper. Draw around the pattern, then cut along the lines you drew, cutting through both layers of paper.

**10.** Use glue to secure the two carpel pieces together, with about 1 inch (2.5 cm) of the green pipe cleaner sandwiched between the pieces, as shown. Allow the glue to dry.

**11.** Fold the red construction paper in half twice. Place the petal pattern on the corner of the folded paper, as shown. Draw around the petal pattern, then cut along the lines you drew, cutting through all four layers of paper. Do not cut through the folded corner. Unfold the paper to form one piece with four connected petals.

**12.** Cut a hole in the centers of the petal and sepal pieces with the paper hole punch.

**13.** Fold the sepals up along the indicated fold lines on the pattern.

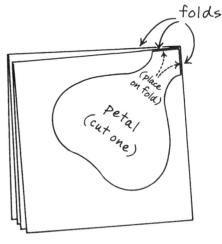

green paper strip

plaster of Paris

folds

(place on fold)

Petal (cut one)

14. Place glue on the top of the receptacle (the strip wrapped around the straw). Insert the straw through the hole in the sepals piece and press the piece against the glue on the receptacle.

15. Place glue on the flat center section of the sepals piece. Then insert the straw through the hole in the petals. Position the piece so that the petals overlap the sepals. Allow the glue to dry.

16. Fold one of the yellow pipe cleaners in half. Insert about 2 inches (5 cm) of the folded end into the straw. Repeat this step with the other yellow pipe cleaner.

17. Insert all of the green pipe cleaner attached to the carpel into the straw so that the carpel is positioned between the yellow pipe cleaners, as shown.

18. Bend about ½ inch (2.5 cm) of each end of the yellow pipe cleaners. Twist the pipe cleaners so that their bent ends point away from the carpel and in different directions.

19. Prepare a legend, such as the one shown, by folding the poster board in half with the short sides together. Draw a picture of the parts in the flower model, number the parts on the drawing, then list the numbered parts.

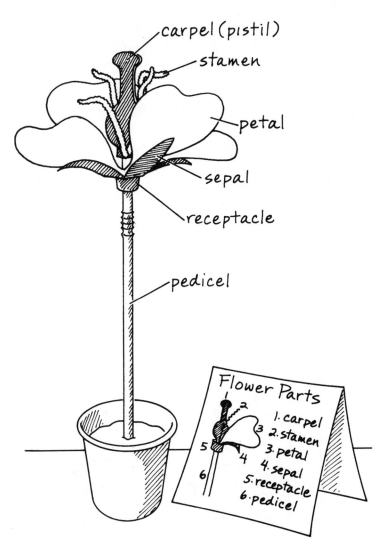

## Results

You have made a model of the parts of a flower.

## Why?

Your model is a **complete flower,** meaning it has these four basic parts: stamens, carpel, petals, and sepals. An **incomplete flower** lacks one or more of the four basic flower parts. In your model, the yellow pipe cleaners represent stamens. The carpel is in the center of the flower, surrounded by several stamens. The red petals surround and protect the carpel and stamens. The sepals are beneath the petals. They surround and protect the petals before the flower opens. The receptacle is represented by the green strip wrapped around the straw. This part of the flower is at the end of the **pedicel** (the flower stem) and supports the flower parts.

## ON YOUR OWN!

1. Display the 3-D flower model by placing it in front of a three-sided backboard. (See Appendix 1 for instructions on making a backboard.) The title of the backboard can be "Flower Parts."

2. Prepare a drawing of a cut-away view of flower parts, such as the ones shown here, with information about each part. Secure the drawings to the backboard using a glue stick. Use string to connect the flower parts to the information sheets.

## BOOK LIST

Forey, Pam. *Wild Flowers of North America.* San Diego: Thunder Bay Press, 1994. More than 20 easy-to-do science projects and facts about flowers, including their parts.

Fustec, Fabienne. *Plants.* New York: Random House, 1993. A simple encyclopedia with information about plants, including facts about flowers.

VanCleave, Janice. *Janice VanCleave's Plants.* New York: Wiley, 1996. Experiments about flower parts and other plant topics. Each chapter contains ideas that can be turned into award-winning science fair projects.

*The Visual Dictionary of Plants.* New York: Dorling Kindersley, 1992. Over 200 photographs and illustrations with information about plants, including flower parts.

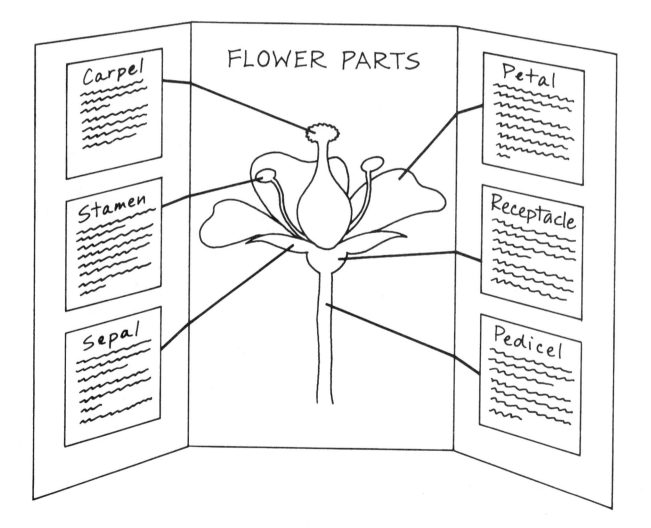

# CHEMISTRY

Oxygen, O

Hydrogen, H

SPRING WATER

Water

Acid

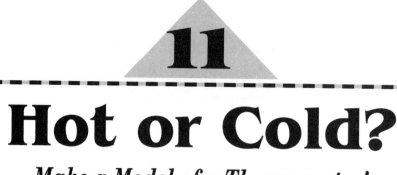

# Hot or Cold?

## Make a Model of a Thermometer!

**Temperature** is a measure of how hot or cold an object is. **Energy** is the ability of an object to cause changes. **Heat** is the energy that flows from a material with a higher temperature to a material with a lower temperature.

**Thermal energy** is the total **kinetic energy, KE** (the energy an object has because of its motion) of the particles making up a material. When a material is hot, its particles move faster than when it is cold. Thus its individual particles have a greater kinetic energy when hot than when cold. The thermal energy (total kinetic energy of the particles) of the material when it is hot is greater than when it is cold. While thermal energy of a material causes its temperature, temperature is not a measure of a material's thermal energy. Instead, thermal energy is the sum of the kinetic energy of all the particles in a material, while temperature is the **average kinetic energy** (thermal energy divided by the total number of particles). For example, a pitcher of lemonade can be the same temperature as a glass of lemonade, because their average kinetic energies are the same. But the pitcher of lemonade has more total thermal energy than the glass of lemonade, because there are more particles in the pitcher than in the glass of lemonade.

A **thermometer** is an instrument that measures the temperature of a material. In 1593, Galileo Galilei (1564–1642) designed the first crude thermometer, which he called a "thermoscope." This thermometer was made from a bulb-shaped glass container about the size of a hen's egg with a narrow tube about 16 inches (40 cm) long. The design of Galileo's thermoscope was based on the fact that gases expand when heated and contract when cooled. Galileo would warm the bulb by squeezing it in his hands, then insert the tube into a container of water. When the bulb cooled, the air inside contracted, and the water rose in the tube to fill the space. The thermoscope did not have a scale, so only **qualitative** (pertaining to the quality or characteristic of something) measurements, such as hot, warm, cool, or very cool, could be made. But even without a scale, Galileo's air thermometer could be used to more accurately compare temperatures of materials than just feeling them could.

Daniel Gabriel Fahrenheit (1686–1736), a German scientist, introduced a thermometer filled with alcohol in 1709, and a thermometer filled with mercury in 1714. He introduced a temperature scale in 1724, which still bears his name. The Fahrenheit scale (F) used today has two reference points, the freezing point (32°F) and boiling point (212°F) of water. The Fahrenheit scale is still widely used in the United States (although seldom in scientific work). The Celsius scale (C) was named for the Swedish astronomer Anders Celsius (1701–1744). The Celsius scale used today has 0° assigned to the freezing point of water and 100° to the boiling point of water. The Kelvin temperature scale (K) was developed by Lord Kelvin (1824–1907) in the mid 1800s. The zero point of this scale is considered the lowest possible temperature of anything in the universe and is about –273°C. At the freezing point of water, the temperature of the Kelvin scale reads 273 K. At the boiling point of water, it reads 373 K. The Celsius and Kelvin scales are widely used by scientists, and the Celsius or Fahrenheit scale is used in daily life. Using scales, **quantitative** (pertaining to the measuring of amounts of something) measurements, such as exact temperatures, can be made.

Many types of thermometers have been used. At one time, the mercury thermometer was the main method of measuring body temperature. It had a narrow section in the tube that stopped liquid mercury from going back into the bulb until the thermometer was shaken. This gave the user time to read the temperature. When mercury was discovered to be a health hazard, other types of thermometers were designed to measure body temperature, such as flexible strips coated with special crystals. The crystals reflect different colors of light depending on the position of their molecules, which change depending on temperature. In liquid-filled thermometers, mercury has been replaced with safe, nontoxic liquids, such as alcohol and a substance like vegetable oil mixed with a dye.

## ACTIVITY: THERMOMETER

### Purpose

To make a model of a liquid-filled thermometer.

## Materials

copy of thermometer pattern on page 46
red crayon
scissors
ruler
pen
transparent tape

## Procedure

1. Use the red crayon to color the liquid strip and the bulb of the thermometer pattern.

2. Cut out the two indicated shaded areas.

3. Cut along the dotted line to separate the liquid strip from the other sections.

4. Score each fold line by laying the ruler along each of the fold lines and then tracing the lines with the pen.

5. Fold the paper along fold line 1, then along fold line 2, and secure the folded sections together with tape.

6. Insert the liquid strip in the liquid strip slot so that the colored side of the strip is visible through the opening in the front of the model.

7. Move the colored strip up and down for different temperatures. The top of the strip lines up with the temperature on the scale.

8. Prepare a flap book containing information about the Celsius scale and how the thermometer works. (See Appendix 5 for instruction on making a flap book.)

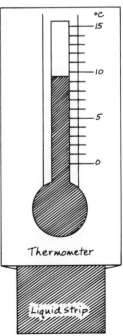

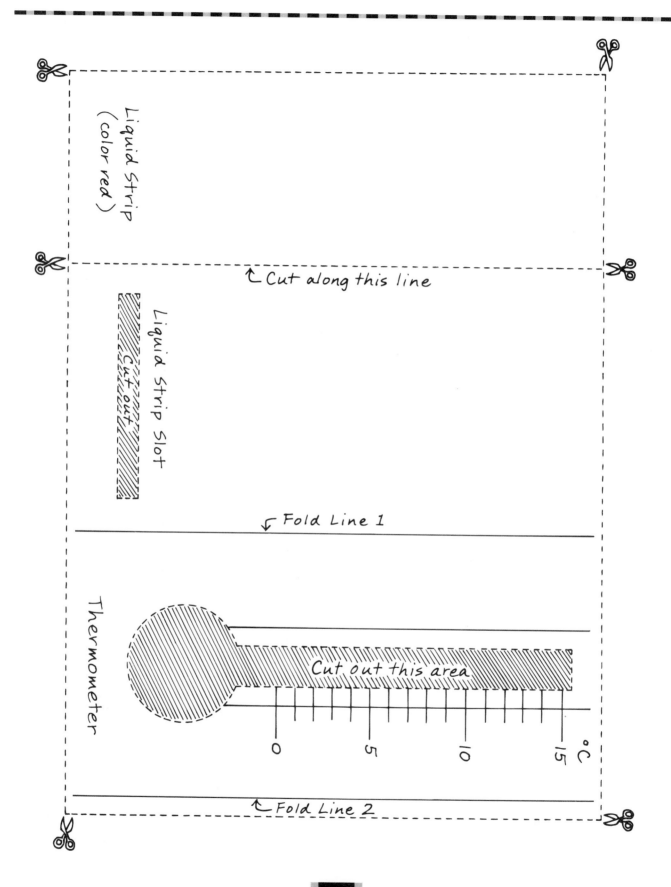

Liquid Strip
(color red)

Cut along this line

Liquid Strip Slot

Cut out

Fold Line 1

Thermometer

Cut out this area

0

5

10

15

°C

Fold Line 2

## Results

You have made a model of a Celsius thermometer.

## Why?

In order to have an enlarged scale, the thermometer model in this experiment represents a portion of a Celsius thermometer instead of a whole thermometer. The thermometer is made of a long tube extending from a bulb with liquid inside the bulb and tube. When the liquid in the bulb is warmed, it expands and moves up the tube. The reading on the scale gets higher as the temperature increases. When the liquid in the bulb is cooled, it contracts and moves down the tube. As the temperature decreases, the reading on the scale decreases. For the scale on the model, each division has a value of 1 degree Celsius (1°C). So a point halfway between two divisions has a value of half a degree, which can be written 0.5°C.

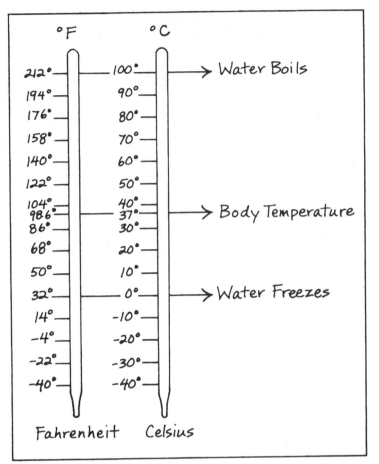

## ON YOUR OWN!

1. Make a tent stand to support the thermometer. (See Appendix 7 for instructions on making a tent stand.)

2. Display the thermometer model in front of a three-paneled backboard. (See Appendix 1 for instructions on making a three-paneled backboard.) In the center panel of the backboard, make drawings of a Celsius and a Fahrenheit thermometer that compare the scales of the two thermometers, as shown here. Some common temperatures, such as the **freezing point** (the temperature at which a liquid **freezes**—changes to a solid) and boiling point (the temperature at which vaporization occurs throughout the liquid)

of water as well as body temperature, can be labeled on the scales.

## BOOK LIST

Chaloner, Jack. *Hot and Cold.* New York: Raintree Steck-Vaughn, 1997. Simple activities that introduce the concepts of hot and cold and explore temperatures at different regions of Earth.

Gardner, Robert, and Eric Kemer. *Science Projects about Temperature and Heat.* Springfield, N.J.: Enslow, 1994. Simple experiments about thermometers and other heat-related topics.

VanCleave, Janice. *Janice VanCleave's Weather.* New York: Wiley, 1995. Experiments about temperature and other weather topics. Each chapter contains ideas that can be turned into award-winning science fair projects.

Walpole, Brenda, et al. *Temperature.* Milwaukee: Gareth Stevens, 1995. Facts and activities about temperature, including the history of the development of the thermometer.

# Different Kinds

## Make a Model of Atoms and Molecules!

**Matter** is anything that occupies space and has **mass** (an amount of matter making up a material). Matter is the stuff that makes up the universe. The term **substance** is used by scientists to mean a basic part of matter. A substance is made of one kind of matter—an element or a compound. A chemical is a substance or mixture of substances.

An **element** is a substance that cannot be broken down into simpler substances by ordinary means. Elements are made of only one kind of **atom,** which is the smallest building block of an element that retains the properties of the element. For example, the element gold is made of gold atoms, oxygen is made of oxygen atoms, and so on. Atoms are so small that about 150 billion atoms could fit on the period at the end of this sentence. There are more than one hundred different elements that have been identified. Elements that occur in nature are called **natural elements.** Carbon, oxygen, nitrogen, and mercury are natural elements. **Synthetic elements** are those made by scientists in a laboratory. Synthetic elements include californium, plutonium, nobelium, einsteinium, and unnilpentium.

**Symbols** for most elements consist of one or two letters. Several new synthetic elements have three letters. If the symbol consists of one letter, it is capitalized, such as C for the element carbon. If the symbol consists of two letters, the first letter is capitalized and the second is lowercase, such as Hg for mercury. Elements with three letters have a capital letter and two lowercase letters, such as Unp for the element unnilpentium.

A **compound** is a substance in which the atoms of two or more elements combine in a certain ratio. There are two types of compounds, molecular compounds and ionic compounds. Like molecules are the building blocks of a **molecular compound.** A **molecule** (a particle made of two or more atoms) is the smallest particle of a molecular compound that can exist independently and still have the properties of the compound. Sucrose, commonly called table sugar, is a molecular compound made of sucrose molecules.

Some elements exist as **diatomic molecules** (molecules of two like or unlike atoms). For example, the symbol for the element hydrogen is H, but hydrogen exists naturally as a diatomic molecule. The **formula** (combination of symbols of elements used to represent a molecule) for diatomic hydrogen is $H_2$. The small 2 following and slightly below the H indicates that there are two atoms of hydrogen linked together.

An **ion** is an atom or group of atoms with a positive or negative charge. **Ionic compounds** are made of **cations** (positive ions) and **anions** (negative ions). Sodium chloride, commonly called table salt, is an ionic compound made up of sodium cations and chloride anions.

A compound has different properties than the elements it is made of. For example, the element sodium is a solid that reacts violently with water, and the element chlorine is a poisonous gas. When these two elements combine forming a compound, the compound is a solid white crystal of harmless table salt, sodium chloride.

## Some Compounds and Their Formulas

| Common Name | Chemical Name | Chemical Formula |
|---|---|---|
| Baking powder | Sodium bicarbonate | $NaHCO_3$ |
| Table sugar | Sucrose | $C_{12}H_{22}O_{11}$ |
| Table salt | Sodium chloride | $NaCl$ |
| Stannous fluoride | Tin(II) fluoride | $SnF_2$ |
| Vinegar | Acetic acid | $HC_2H_3O_2$ |
| Water | Water | $H_2O$ |

Sodium Chloride Crystal
(an ionic compound)

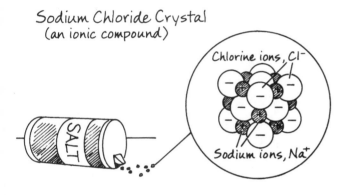

Water
(a molecular compound)

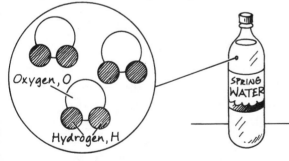

## ACTIVITY: SINGLE AND CONNECTED

### Purpose

To make models of atoms and molecules.

## Materials

two lemon-size pieces of modeling clay of different colors—1 red, 1 yellow
ruler
pen
1 sheet of copy paper
two crayons—1 red, 1 yellow
toothpicks

## Procedure

1. Divide the red clay into four equal parts. Shape each clay piece into a ball. Each part represents an atom of hydrogen.

2. Divide the yellow clay into three equal parts. Shape each clay piece into a ball. Each part represents an atom of oxygen.

3. Use the ruler, pen, and copy paper to prepare a matter data table, such as the one shown on page 50.

4. In the data table, make a colored drawing of each of the two kinds of atoms, hydrogen (red clay ball) and oxygen (yellow clay ball).

| Matter Data | | | |
| --- | --- | --- | --- |
| **Atoms** | | | |
| hydrogen ● | | oxygen ○ | |
| **Molecules** | | | |
| **Name** | **Formula** | **Structure** | **Model** |
| Hydrogen (diatomic) | $H_2$ | H—H | |
| Oxygen (diatomic) | $O_2$ | O=O | |
| Water | $H_2O$ | O H H | |

**5.** Form molecules using the clay balls for atoms and toothpicks for bonds. The structures listed in the table here indicate the number and location of the bonds between the atoms. For example, there are double bonds between the oxygen atoms in an oxygen molecule.

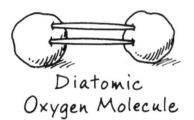

Diatomic Oxygen Molecule

**6.** In the "Model" column of the table, make a colored drawing of each kind of molecule.

## Results

You have made models of atoms and molecules and described the models on a data sheet.

## Why?

The individual clay balls represent atoms, and each kind of clay ball "atom" differs from other types of clay ball "atoms" by its size and/or color. Clay ball "molecules" are made up of clay ball "atoms" linked by toothpicks that represent bonds. Some of the molecules are made of two atoms of the same kind and represent diatomic molecules. The water molecule is made of two different kinds of atoms and represents a molecular compound.

## ON YOUR OWN!

**1.** Make models of other molecules, such as those in the "Simple Molecules to Make" table on page 51. Prepare a matter data table and make models of those molecules. You can find the name, formula, and structure of other molecules in a chemistry textbook.

**2.** Prepare information sheets for the two types of models—atoms and molecules. For example, on the atom sheet, title the sheet "Atom," draw a diagram of one of the clay atoms, then write about atoms in general, including information about elements and diatomic elements. Include a definition of an

| Simple Molecules to Make | | |
|---|---|---|
| Name | Formula | Structure |
| Carbon dioxide | $CO_2$ | O=C=O |
| Chlorine | $Cl_2$ | Cl–Cl |
| Fluorine | $F_2$ | F–F |
| Nitrogen | $N_2$ | N≡N |

atom and give examples. Prepare a similar sheet on molecules. These sheets, as well as the matter data table prepared in the original experiment, can be matted and displayed on a three-sided backboard. The data table can be in the center with one information sheet on either side panel. See Appendix 1 for instructions on making a three-paneled backboard and Appendix 6 for instructions on matting. Your atom and molecule models can be displayed in front of the backboard.

## BOOK LIST

Chrisholm, Jane, and Mary Johnson. *Introduction to Chemistry.* London: Usborne, 1990. Basic chemistry topics, including molecular models.

Nye, Bill. *Bill Nye the Science Guy's Big Blast of Science.* New York: Addison-Wesley, 1993. Fun science experiments and information including atoms and molecules.

VanCleave, Janice. *Janice VanCleave's Molecules.* New York: Wiley, 1993. Experiments about molecular models and other molecule topics. Each chapter contains ideas that can be turned into award-winning science fair projects.

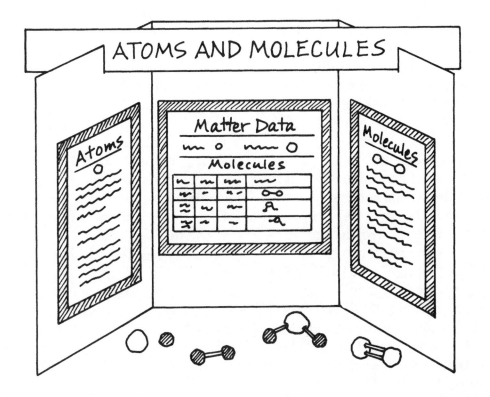

# 13

# Different Forms

*Make a Model of the States of Matter!*

**Physical properties** are characteristics of a substance that can be measured and/or observed without changing the makeup of the substance. Physical properties of matter include state, size, color, and taste.

The form in which matter exists is an important physical property of matter. The three common forms of matter on Earth, called **states of matter,** are solid, liquid, and gas. The state of a substance depends on the motion of its particles (atoms, molecules, or ions). The particles in **solids** are very close.

The arrangement of particles forming most **solids** is a regular, repeating pattern with flat surfaces called a **crystal lattice.** Solids made up of crystal lattices are called **crystalline solids.** For example, when liquid water freezes, the water molecules link together, forming crystal lattices. A large piece of ice is made up of many small crystal lattices that fit together like a puzzle. The shape of a crystalline solid depends on the arrangements of the particles within its crystal lattices.

The forces between the particles in crystalline solids act like springs, keeping the particles in relatively the same position with only slight vibration. The "springs" restrict the particles from being pushed closer together or pulled farther apart. Because of this arrangement, these particles cannot move far out of place or flow over or around one another. This means that a crystalline solid has a definite shape and **volume** (the amount of space an object occupies).

There are a few solids, however, in which the particles lack an ordered internal structure. Instead their particles generally are chainlike structures that can be tangled and twisted instead of stacked in a rigid structure of repeating patterns. Because the particle structure is not rigid as are crystalline solids, the particles can slowly flow around one another and thus do not keep a definite shape. Solids that are **noncrystalline** (not made of crystal lattices) are called **amorphous solids.** Rubber, plastic, and even glass are amorphous solids. While glass is rigid to the touch, it is like a very slow-moving liquid. The movement of the particles in glass takes many years. If you look through the windows in a very old house, you'll find it more difficult to see through the glass at the bottom than at the top. This is because over time, due to the downward pull of gravity, the glass particles have flowed slowly downward, making the windowpane thicker at the bottom and thinner at the top.

The particles in **liquids** are more loosely bound together and can slide past each other. So liquid particles move more freely than do solids. Some liquids flow more freely than others. The measure of how fast a liquid flows is called **viscosity** (the measure of how fast a liquid flows). Honey flows slowly and is said to have a high **viscosity,** while water, which flows quickly, has a low viscosity. Since particles in a liquid are free to move in any direction, liquids have no definite shape but they do have a definite volume. If you pour a quart of water into a square container, the liquid takes the shape of a square, but if you pour it into a round container, it becomes round. However, in both containers, regardless of shape, the volume of the water, which is one quart, remains the same.

The third state of matter is **gas,** in which the particles move very quickly in all directions. The gas particles are in constant motion, constantly hitting each other, the walls of their container, and anything in their path. Gases have no definite volume or shape. A gas takes the volume and shape of the container it is placed in. Gas particles can be pushed close together. When you blow up a balloon, for example, you squeeze a large amount of gas into a small space. Gas particles can also easily spread out. For example, the smell of baking cookies can be smelled throughout the house because the gases given off by the cookies spread out and fill the house. The term **vapor** is used for the gaseous state of a substance that is normally in a liquid or solid state.

A **physical change** is one in which the physical properties of a substance may be changed, but the particles making up the substance are not changed. Melting, freezing, evaporation, and condensation are examples of physical changes. When heated, solids, such as ice, **melt** (change to a liquid) and liquids, such as water, **evaporate** (change to a gas at the liquid's surface). When cooled, gases, such as water vapor, **condense** (change to a liquid) and liquids, such as water, freeze (change to a solid).

## ACTIVITY: FIRM

### Purpose

To model the solid state of matter.

### Materials

glue
two 20-by-28-inch (50-by-70-cm) pieces of poster board
yardstick (meterstick)
pen
scissors
marker
8-by-8-inch (20-by-20-cm) square piece of poster board
three crayons—1 yellow, 1 blue, 1 green
transparent tape
56-inch (140-cm) piece of string
six unlined index cards—2 yellow, 2 blue, 2 green
paper hole punch

### Procedure

1. Use the 20-by-28-inch (50-by-70-cm) pieces of poster board to prepare a three-sided backboard with a title strip. (See Appendix 1 for instructions on making the backboard.)

Solid $\xrightarrow{\text{melts}}$ $\xleftarrow{\text{freezes}}$ Liquid $\xrightarrow{\text{evaporates}}$ $\xleftarrow{\text{condenses}}$ Gas

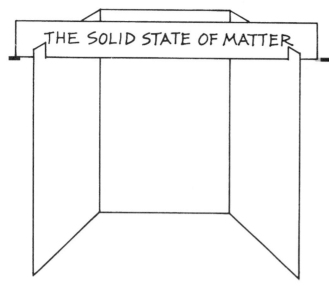

Make the notches for the title strip 1 inch (2.5 cm) from the edge of the side panels.

**2.** Use the marker to label the title strip "The Solid State of Matter."

**3.** Cut the string into seven 8-inch (20-cm) pieces.

**4.** Use the 8-by-8-inch (20-by-20-cm) square piece of poster board and one 8-inch (20-cm) piece of string to make a hanging poster board pyramid. (See Appendix 9, Part D, for instructions on making the hanging pyramid.) Note: Before taping the sides of the pyramid together, use the crayons to color triangle A yellow, triangle C blue, and triangle D green. Use the marker to label the three colored sides of the pyramid: yellow, "Types"; blue, "Inside"; green, "Examples".

**6.** Use tape to attach the string of the pyramid to the center of the backboard title strip.

**7.** Use the paper hole punch to cut a hole in the center at one of the short sides of each index card.

**8.** Label one of the yellow cards "Crystalline" and the other "Amorphous." On each card, print a general physical description of each type of solid.

**9.** Use the paper hole punch to cut two holes at the bottom edge of the hanging pyramid, each about 2.5 inches (6.25 cm) from either corner of the yellow side (labeled "Atoms"). Taking a piece of string, tie one end of the string in the hole in the pyramid and the other end in the hole in one of the yellow cards. Repeat, using the other yellow card.

**10.** Repeat steps 8 and 9, using the blue cards and blue side of the pyramid. Print a description of the internal structure of the two types of solids. Draw an example of the internal structure of each type of solid at the bottom of each card.

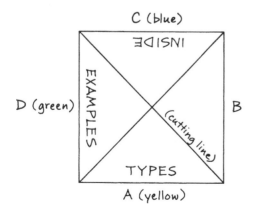

**5.** Tape the string to Triangle B. Overlap Triangle B with Triangle A and tape together.

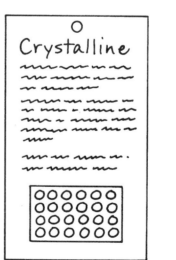

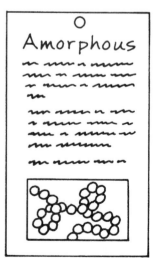

**11.** Repeat steps 8 and 9, using the green cards and green side of the pyramid. Print a list of examples of the two types of solids. Draw diagrams of the examples at the bottom of each card.

## Results

You have made a model of the solid state of matter.

## Why?

The pyramid shows the solid state of matter. The colored cards hanging from the pyramid describe the two types of solid states, crystalline and amorphous. The cards also show the general description, the internal structure, and examples of the two basic types of solids.

## ON YOUR OWN!

Make a model of water at three states of matter. The title of the model could be "Water States," and the three colored sides of the pyramid each could be labeled with one of the states of matter: yellow, "Solid"; blue, "Liquid"; green, "Gas." Prepare a colored thermometer card for each state, showing water's freezing point (the temperature at which a substance freezes) for ice, room temperature for liquid water, and water's **boiling point** (the temperature at which vaporization occurs throughout a liquid) for vapor.

Two additional cards can be hung from each side of the pyramid. A physical description of the state of matter can be printed on one card. On the other card, use drawings, pictures, and/or lists of materials that are typically found in that state of matter. For example, solids might include a pencil, a book, an apple, a rock, and ice. Liquids might include milk, soda, and water. For gases, you could draw the sky and label it with a list of the gases in air (nitrogen, oxygen, carbon dioxide, and water vapor).

## BOOK LIST

Science and Technology Department of the Carnegie Library of Pittsburgh. *The Handy Science Answer Book.* New York: Visible Ink, 1997. A book of science questions and answers, including some about the phases of matter.

Strauss, Michael. *Where Puddles Go.* Portsmouth, N.H.: Heinemann, 1995. A book of chemistry experiments and activities, including some on the phases of matter.

VanCleave, Janice. *Janice Van Cleave's Chemistry for Every Kid.* New York: Wiley, 1989. Fun, simple chemistry experiments, including information about phases of matter.

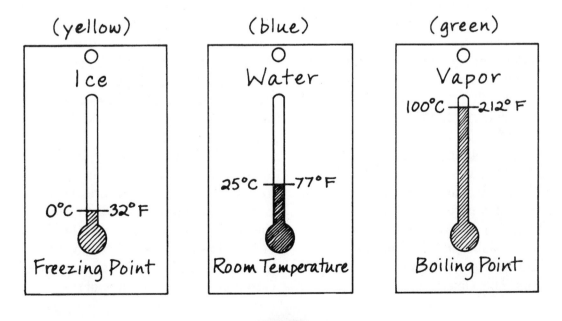

# How Much?

## *Make a Model of Metric Measuring!*

Measures are standard units used to express specific quantities, such as **length** (the distance from one point to another), volume, and mass. Systems of measures developed gradually and were different in different civilizations. Counting might be considered the earliest form of measurement. In prehistoric times, certain quantities of different products were used in trading. For example, a lamb might be traded for 20 handfuls of grain. This simple barter system lasted for thousands of years.

It is believed that the first uses of linear measurements took place between 10000 and 8000 B.C. These early systems were based on natural objects. One of the earliest-known units of length measurements is the cubit. This measure was used by the Egyptians, Sumerians, Babylonians, and Hebrews. A **cubit** is the distance between the elbow and the tip of the middle finger. A **span** is the distance from the tip of the thumb to the tip of the little finger of an outstretched hand. The Greeks introduced the length measurement of a **foot** (modern length measurement equal to 12 inches). The foot measurement was usually divided into 16 fingers. Later the Romans divided the foot unit into 12 parts called *uncias*. The English word *inch* comes from this word. The width of a man's thumb was equal to 1 uncia and the length of a man's foot was 1 foot.

The problem with using measurements equal to the length of body parts is that the body parts on different people can be different sizes. So, the cubit, foot, or uncia measured by one person might be different from those measured by another person. This caused great confusion, errors, and disputes in the trading between civilizations as well as among the locals in marketplaces. In 1305, King Edward I of England made a royal order that established standard measurements called the **imperial system.** Until the nineteenth century, each imperial standard was made into an iron bar and kept in London. Brass or bronze copies were sent to other towns. The British imperial system was used by the U.S. colonies and is the system from which the United States's current system of weights and measurement was derived.

In 1791, French scientists measured the distance from the North Pole to the equator as accurately as possible, and divided this distance into 10 million parts. One part was called a **meter,** or measure. **Volume** is the amount of space an object occupies. The **cubic centimeter (cm$^3$)** is a common metric volume unit determined by multiplying length × width × height measured in centimeters. A container with dimensions of 10 by 10 by 10 centimeters has a volume of 1,000 cm$^3$, which was called a **liter.** The mass of 1 cm$^3$ of water was called a **gram** (the basic metric unit of mass). The table shown here lists the common metric units and their prefixes.

In 1840 the metric system became mandatory in France, and it has remained so ever since. The use of the metric system spread slowly to other European countries. In 1866 the metric system was made legal but not mandatory in the United States. However, the United States mainly uses a system called the English system, which is closely related to the imperial system.

| Metric Units | | | |
|---|---|---|---|
| Prefix | Length | Volume | Mass |
| | Meter, m | Liter, L | Gram, g |
| milli, m | 1 mm (0.001m) | 1 mL (0.001 L) | 1 mg (0.001g) |
| centi, c | 1 cm (0.01 m) | 1 cL (0.01 L) | 1 cg (0.01 g) |
| deci, d | 1 dm (0.1 m) | 1 dL (0.1 L) | 1 dg (0.1 g) |
| kilo, k | 1 km (1,000 m) | 1 kL (1,000 L) | 1 kg (1,000 g) |

The metric system was used by scientists until 1960, when a revised system based on the metric system was established. The new system, called the **SI (International System),** is used for scientific work in many countries, including the United States.

## ACTIVITY: FULL UP

## Purpose

To model the metric volume of 1 liter.

## Materials

metric ruler
pen
32-by-32-cm piece of white poster board
scissors
baking pan
1,000-mL measuring cup
tap water

## Procedure

1. Use the ruler and pen to draw a 30-by-30-cm square on the poster board. Mark the dashed and solid lines shown in the diagram, dividing the square into nine 10-by-10-cm squares. The square is a metric box pattern. Label the squares as shown.

2. Use the scissors to cut out the metric box pattern.

3. Fold the poster board along one of the fold lines on the pattern and crease the fold by pressing it with your fingers. Then unfold the poster board, and repeat folding along each fold line.

4. Now cut along the fold lines only where shown.

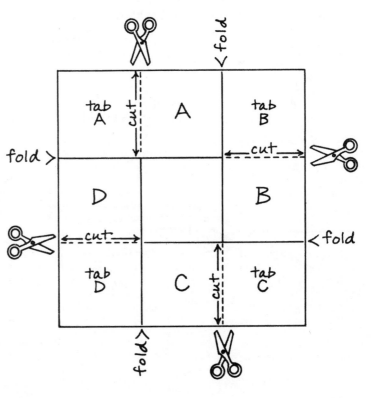

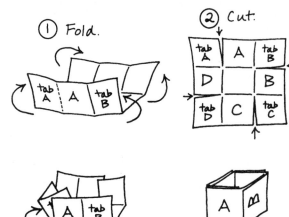

① Fold.

② Cut.

| tab A | A | tab B |
|---|---|---|
| D | | B |
| tab D | C | tab C |

③ Fold tab A behind side A and glue.

④ Continue to fold and glue.

5. Glue tab A to the back of side A. Then glue tab B to side B. Continue gluing the tabs and sides together until a box is formed.

6. On the inside of the box, cover the seams with a thin line of glue.

7. Allow the glue to dry.

8. Place the box in the baking pan. Then fill the measuring cup to the 1,000-mL mark with water and slowly pour the water into the box.

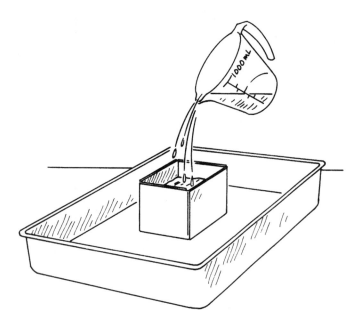

## Results

You have made a box with a volume of 1,000 cubic centimeters. The box holds exactly one thousand milliliters of water.

## Why?

The volume of a box is measured by multiplying its length × width × height. The box you made is 10 centimeters on each side, so its volume is 1,000 cubic centimeters, or $cm^3$ (10 cm × 10 cm × 10 cm). Volume is also measured in liters or portions of liters. One milliliter (mL) is the same volume as 1 $cm^3$. This means that 1,000 $cm^3$ is the same as 1,000 mL. Since 1,000 mL equals 1 liter, you've shown with your box that 1,000 $cm^3$ = 1 liter.

## ON YOUR OWN!

The metric box can be displayed in front of a three-sided backboard. Information sheets about the three common measurements of length, volume, and mass can be matted and displayed on the backboard. (See Appendix 1 for instructions on making a three-sided backboard and Appendix 6 for instructions on matting.) The title of the display can be "Metric Measurements." Since the metric box models volume, place information about volume on the center panel of the display board and place the box on the table in front of that panel. Put information about length on one side panel, and about mass on the other. Diagrams and information about each measurement can include:

- **Length:** Give a definition of length and the fact that the basic metric unit of length is the meter (m). Display a meter stick or metric ruler in front of this section of the backboard.

- **Volume:** Give a definition of volume and explain that two common metric volume units are the cubic centimeter (cm³) and the liter (L). Point out that a volume measured in cubic centimeters is determined by multiplying length × width × height measured in centimeters. Indicate that 1,000 cm³ = 1 L. Display the metric box as an example of volume.

- **Mass:** Give information about the comparison of weight and mass. For example, the **weight** of an object is the measure of the force of **gravity** (the force of attraction between objects due to their mass) while its mass depends on the amount of matter it is made of. The basic metric unit of mass is the gram (g) and the basic metric unit of weight is the **newton** (N). A **balance** is an instrument used to measure mass by comparing one mass with another. Display a balance or a stand-up card with a picture of a balance that measures in grams in front of this section of the backboard. Scientific catalogs have pictures of balances that can be photocopied.

## BOOK LIST

Kenda, Margaret, and Phyllis S. Williams. *Math Wizardry for Kids.* Hauppauge, N.Y.: Barrons, 1995. Puzzles, games, and fun activities about measuring and other math topics.

VanCleave, Janice. *Janice VanCleave's Math for Every Kid.* New York: Wiley, 1991. Fun, simple measuring investigations and other math topics.

Walpole, Brenda, et al. *Measure Up with Science: Distance.* Milwaukee: Gareth Stevens Publishing. Fun activities and facts about the history of measuring.

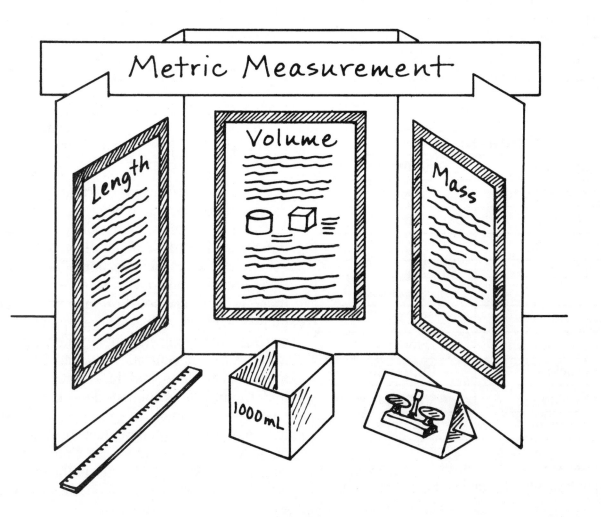

# More or Less?

## *Make a Model of Acids and Bases!*

Acids and bases are two different types of chemicals. **Acids** contain hydrogen. When an acid is added to water, it breaks up into positive and negative ions. The positive ion is always a hydrogen ion, $H^+$. The hydrogen ions quickly combine with water molecules, producing **hydronium ions** ($H_3O^+$). **Bases,** also called **alkalis,** contain oxygen and hydrogen. In water, bases break up into positive and negative ions. The negative ions produced are always **hydroxide ions ($OH^{-1}$).** The table shows some common acids. Some acids are found in foods and drinks, such as lemons, vinegar, and sodas. Acids have a sour taste.

| Common Acids | |
|---|---|
| **Name** | **Found In** |
| Acetylsalicylic acid | Aspirin |
| Acetic acid | Vinegar |
| Carbonic acid | Sodas |
| Citric acid | Citrus fruits, such as lemons |
| Boric acid | Eye wash |
| Hydrochloric acid | Stomach |
| Lactic acid | Buttermilk |
| Maleic acid | Apples |
| Sulfuric acid | Battery |

Bases can dissolve fats and oils, so they are used in household cleaners. Some bases can dissolve hair, which makes them useful for cleaning clogged bathroom drains. This table shows some common bases and their uses.

| Common Bases | |
|---|---|
| **Name** | **Found In** |
| Aluminum hydroxide | Deodorant, antacid |
| Ammonium hydroxide | Household cleaner, glass cleaner |
| Magnesium hydroxide | Laxative, antacid |
| Sodium hydroxide | Drain cleaner, soap ingredient |

Acids and bases can be harmful, but many are found in foods and medicines. Whether an acid or a base is harmful or not depends on its **concentration** (the amount of matter per unit volume), which is an indication of how much acid or base is mixed with water. A concentrated acid or base **solution** (a mixture that is uniformly blended) has a large amount of acid or base and a small amount of water. To increase the concentration of an acidic solution, more acid is added, and thus there are more hydronium ions as compared to water molecules in the solution. To increase the concentration of a basic solution, more base is added, and thus there are more hydroxide ions as compared to water molecules in the solution. To decrease the concentration, the acid or base

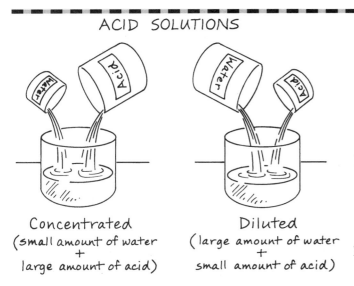

ACID SOLUTIONS

Concentrated
(small amount of water
+
large amount of acid)

Diluted
(large amount of water
+
small amount of acid)

solution is **diluted,** meaning water is added. In a dilute solution of acid or base, there is a large amount of water molecules as compared to the hydronium ions or hydroxide ions in the solution.

The special scale for measuring the acidic or basic nature of a substance is called the **pH scale.** The values on the pH scale range from 0 to 14, with the pH value of 7 being **neutral** (having no acidic or basic properties). Water has a pH value of 7. Acids have a pH of less than 7 and bases have a pH greater than 7. The pH of a solution can be determined with an instrument called a pH meter or by using an **indicator** (a chemical that changes color in an acid and/or a base). For example, blue litmus turns red in an acid solution and red litmus turns blue in a basic solution.

## ACTIVITY: HIGH AND LOW

### Purpose

To model a pH scale.

### Materials

fine-point black marker
14-by-24-inch (32.5-by-60-cm) piece of
   white poster board
yardstick (meter stick)

pen
crayons (optional)
scissors

## Procedure

1. Use the marker and the measuring stick to draw a line from top to bottom and 3 inches (7.5 cm) from one of the long sides on the poster board.

2. With the vertical line on the left, draw 15 horizontal lines 1½ inch apart starting at the vertical line.

3. Starting with the second horizontal line, number the lines 1 through 14, as shown.

4. Use the marker to add the title "pH Scale" at the top of the poster board.

5. Use the marker to add the labels "Neutral," "Acidic Concentration," "Basic Concentration," and arrows as shown.

6. Draw and color items from the table, "pH Values of Some Common Substances," or cut out pictures of the items from magazines.

7. Use lifters to attach the drawings of each product to the poster board at the correct pH. (See Appendix 8 for instructions for making lifters.) Place the products so that they are evenly distributed on the pH scale model.

## Results

You have made a pH model showing some common substances and their pH values.

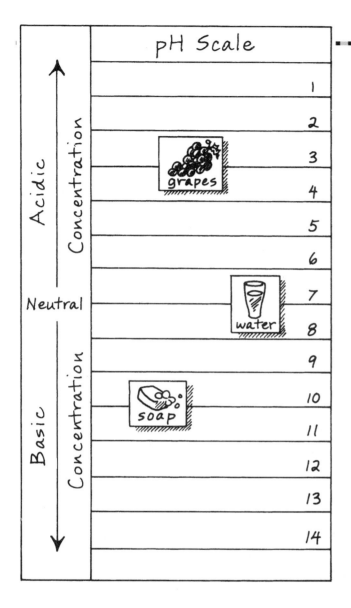

## Why?

As the pH value of a substance decreases, its acidic value increases. Thus, the lower the pH number, the more concentrated the acid. An increase in the pH value of a substance is an increase in the basic properties of the substance. Thus, the higher the pH number, the more concentrated the base.

## ON YOUR OWN!

Prepare information sheets for the two types of chemicals, acids and bases. For example, title one sheet "Acid." Give a definition of the term *acid,* and give examples of strong and weak acids. Acids and bases may be classified as strong or weak depending on how well they break up when added to water. Generally, a strong acid or base breaks up completely into ions when added to water. Thus a strong acid in water has more hydronium ions than does a weak acid. A strong base in water has more hydronium ions than does a weak base. Include information about the pH of acids as well as how to test for the presence of acids. Prepare a similar sheet on bases. These sheets can be matted and displayed on a three-sided backboard. The pH model can be secured to the center panel of the backboard with the acid and base information sheets on either side panel. See Appendix 1 for instructions on making a three-sided backboard with a title strip and Appendix 6 for instructions on matting.

## BOOK LIST

Churchill, E. Richard, Louis V. Loesching, and Muriel Mandell. 365 *Simple Science Experiments with Everyday Materials.* New York: Black Dog & Leventhal, 1997. Easy science experiments, including those about acids and bases.

VanCleave, Janice. *Janice VanCleave's Chemistry for Every Kid.* New York: Wiley, 1989. Fun, simple chemistry experiments, including information about acids and bases.

| pH Values of Common Products | | | |
|---|---|---|---|
| **Name** | **pH** | **Name** | **pH** |
| Stomach acid | 1 | Water | 7 |
| Lemon | 2 | Eggs | 8 |
| Grapes | 3 | Baking Soda | 9 |
| Tomato | 4 | Soap | 10 |
| Banana | 5 | Cleaning ammonia | 12 |
| Milk | 6 | Lye | 14 |

# IV

# EARTH SCIENCE

melting, then cooling

metamorphic

igneous

heat and pressure

weathering and compaction and cementation

sedimentary

# Changing

## *Make a Model of Seasons!*

Latitude is distance in degrees north or south of the equator. The equator is an imaginary line around Earth at 0° latitude that divides Earth into northern and southern halves. The **temperate zones** are the two regions between latitudes 23.5° and 66.5° north and south of the equator. In these areas, yearly temperatures average between −13°F and 100°F (−25°C and 38°C). This change in temperature is due to the position of Earth during its orbit (the curved path of one body around another) around the Sun, which results in **climatic seasons** (divisions of the year based on temperature changes). In most of the temperate zone, there are four separate climatic seasons: spring, summer, autumn, and winter. Each season lasts about three months and has different weather conditions. During the **spring,** the days are warm and the nights are cool. **Summer** follows with hot days and warm nights. In **autumn,** days and nights become cooler, similar to those in spring, leading to cold **winter** days and nights.

Climatic seasons are a result of changes in the amount of sunlight that reaches an area on Earth, which affects temperature. Direct rays of sunlight are perpendicular to the Earth's surface, meaning the rays are at a 90° angle to the surface. Direct rays provide the greatest concentration of light in an area. For example, if you hold a flashlight perpendicular to a sheet of paper, the direct light forms a bright, round circle of light on the paper. If the paper is tilted away from the flashlight, the circle of light spreads into an oval covering more of the paper.

While the same amount of light hits the paper, the oval of light is dimmer because the light is spread over a larger area.

The amount of sunlight hitting an area of Earth's surface depends on the position of Earth in relation to the Sun. Since the Earth's axis is at a tilt of about 23½° in relation to its orbit around the Sun, the poles of Earth tilt toward the Sun for part of the year and away from the Sun for part of the year. In the Northern Hemisphere, the **summer solstice** (the first day of summer) is when the North Pole is tilted toward the Sun, which occurs on or about June 21, as shown in position A in the diagram.

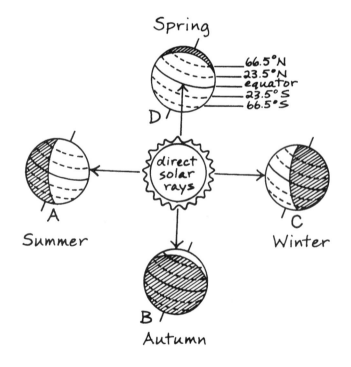

Seasons in the Northern Hemisphere

64

The Sun's rays on this day are directly on the Tropic of Cancer, thus the Sun's apparent path in the sky is at its highest for regions in the Northern Hemisphere. The higher the Sun's path, the more direct are its rays and the longer are the days.

As Earth moves in its orbit from position A to position B, the Sun's path becomes lower in the sky and the days shorten. On or about September 23, on the **autumn equinox** (the first day of autumn), neither pole is tilted toward the Sun. On this day the Sun's rays are direct at the equator and because of the curved shape of Earth, as one moves away from the equator, the angle of the Sun's rays increases, with the greatest angle being at the poles. So, while on this date all places on Earth have equal hours of daylight and night, it is hotter at the equator and coldest at the poles.

Continuing its orbit, Earth moves from position B to C. During this time the North Pole tilts farther from the Sun each day, and in the Northern Hemisphere the Sun's path in the sky becomes lower and the days shorter. On or about December 22, the **winter solstice** (the first day of winter) occurs and the Sun's rays shine most directly on the Tropic of Capricorn. In the Northern Hemisphere, the Sun's path is lowest in the sky and it is the shortest day of the year.

As Earth moves from position C to D, the Sun's path rises a little higher in the sky each day, and each day is a little longer. On or about March 21, the **spring equinox** (the first day of spring), as on the autumnal equinox, neither pole is tilted toward the Sun. Again, all places on Earth have 12 hours of daylight. As Earth continues its journey, in the Northern Hemisphere each day the Sun's path in the sky is higher and the days are longer. On or about June 21, Earth reaches position A, thus completing its yearly orbit around the Sun, and heads toward position B again.

## ACTIVITY: HALF AND HALF
### Purpose

To make a model of the positions of Earth and the Sun during the summer solstice.

### Materials

two 12-inch (30-cm) bamboo skewers
4-inch (10-cm) diameter Styrofoam ball
6-inch (15-cm) diameter Styrofoam ball
lemon-size piece of modeling clay
paint brush
acrylic paints in yellow and black
black marker
measuring stick
pencil
22-by-22-inch (55-by-55-cm) piece of white poster board
protractor

### Procedure

1. Carefully insert a bamboo skewer through the center of each Styrofoam ball.

2. Divide the clay in half and make a ball out of each piece. Using one of the clay balls, make a stand by pressing the ball of clay against a table. Then insert the pointed end of the skewer that is stuck through the large ball into the clay stand. Repeat with the second piece of clay and the skewer stuck through the small ball.

3. Use the brush to paint the large ball yellow. This is a Sun model.

4. With the skewer through the small ball standing vertically, use the marker to draw a line around the ball midway between the top and bottom. This line represents Earth's equator.

5. Draw a second line around the ball, starting 1 cm to the left of the skewer at the top of the ball and ending 1 cm to the right of the skewer at the bottom. This line represents

the boundary between day and night on Earth.

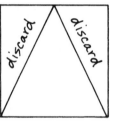

6. Use the brush to paint the left side of the day/night boundary line black, as shown. This is the Earth model.

7. Use the measuring stick and pencil to draw two diagonal lines on the poster board from two adjacent corners to the center of the opposite side, as shown. Cut along the lines, keeping the large center triangle.

8. Use the marker to print the title "Summer Solstice: Northern Hemisphere" on the poster board. Below the title on the card, draw a diagram of Earth's position in its orbit about the Sun, as shown.

9. Stand the Earth model about 3 inches from the left bottom corner of the poster board triangle. Stand the protractor in the clay stand with the vertical skewer in line with 90° on the protractor. Then tilt the skewer 23½° to the right.

10. Stand the Sun model to the right of the Earth model and about 3 inches from the right corner of the poster board triangle.

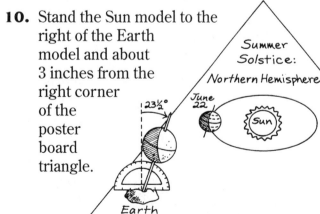

## Results

You have made a model of the summer solstice in the Northern Hemisphere.

## Why?

Because Earth's axis is tilted in relation to the Sun, during the summer solstice, direct sun rays hit the Tropic of Cancer. As Earth rotates, the Northern Hemisphere stays in the light longer. The result is the longest day of the year.

## ON YOUR OWN!

Design a **diorama** (a 3-D miniature scene with figures placed in front of a painted background) that displays the characteristics of summer. The display background can be a pyramid made with a 22-by-22-inch (55-by-55-cm) square piece of white poster board. (See Appendix 9 for instructions for making a pyramid.) Turn the pyramid on one side so that one triangle forms the floor and the two other triangles form the sides of the display. Put the summer solstice model on the floor of the display. Add drawings on one side of the display to represent the summer season. Include trees with green leaves, activities such as swimming, and people dressed in cool summer clothes. On the other side of the display, attach a data table showing the times of sunrise and sunset during a summer week.

## BOOK LIST

Moche, Dinah. *Astronomy Today.* New York: Random House, 1995. Information about planets, stars, and space exploration, including facts about seasons.

VanCleave, Janice. *Janice VanCleave's Geography for Every Kid.* New York: Wiley, 1993. Fun, simple geography experiments, including information about seasons.

Watt, Fiona. *Planet Earth.* London: Usborne, 1991. Information, projects, and activities about Earth, including some about seasons.

# Layers

## Model of Earth's Layers!

Different kinds of chemicals exist at the Earth's surface than at different depths below its surface. The Earth therefore can be described as having layers with different chemical compositions. Earth has three main layers: the core, the mantle, and the crust. The **core** is the center layer and is believed to be made mostly of iron. The core is divided into two layers, the inner core and the outer core. Both layers are about 2,125 miles (3,400 km) thick.

The **mantle** is the middle and the largest layer, with a thickness of about 1,812 miles (2,900 km). The most common chemicals found in this layer are **silicates,** which are made of the elements silicon and oxygen combined with another element. The silicates in this layer are mostly combined with the elements iron and magnesium.

The outermost layer of Earth is the **crust.** The crust is very thin in comparison to the other two layers. It is about 44 miles (70 km) thick in some mountainous regions and less than an average of about 5 miles (8 km) thick under the ocean. Like the mantle, the crust contains large quantities of silicates, but they are mostly combined with aluminum, iron, and magnesium.

Earth can also be divided into layers based on physical states (solids and liquids). The layers of Earth are mostly solid material, even though the temperatures deep within Earth are high enough to melt the substances that make up these materials. This is because of the great pressures within Earth. With depth, temperature and pressure increase. For example, at the surface, some parts of Earth's crust have a temperature of 32°F (0°C) and a pressure of about 14.7 pounds/in$^2$ (1 atm), while at the center of Earth's core, the temperature is believed to be about 9,932°F (5,500°C) with a pressure of 52,920,000 pounds/in$^2$ (3,600,000 atm). At Earth's surface, with a pressure of 14.7 pounds/in$^2$ (1 atm), iron melts at a temperature of 2,800°F (1,538°C), but at the high inner core pressure, the melting point of iron is 11,552°F (6,400°C). Thus iron is solid at Earth's surface and solid in the inner core as well. The balance between temperature and pressure varies with depth within Earth. Based on this balance, Earth has five separate layers. Some of the layers are solid, others are liquid, while others are in between.

- **Inner Core:** The solid inner layer of Earth's core and an area with the greatest pressure and temperature. The diameter of this region is about 750 miles (1,200 km).
- **Outer Core:** The liquid outer layer of Earth's core, where the temperature is high and the pressure is not great enough to make the layer solid. Because Earth rotates, this liquid interior layer moves in a circular motion. The motion of the molten iron and nickel is thought to cause Earth to have a magnetic field. The thickness of this layer is about 1,375 miles (2,200 km).
- **Mesosphere:** A solid layer starting at the boundary of the outer core and making up most of the mantle. The temperature at this depth is not high enough to overcome the great pressure, so the mesosphere is solid.

The thickness of this layer is about 1,638 miles (2,620 km).

- **Athenosphere:** A semisolid layer of Earth that makes up the upper part of the mantle. The balance between temperature and pressure in this layer softens the materials but does not make them liquid. Instead, the materials are in a semisolid state that is in between the liquid and solid phase. This condition is called **plasticity.** The thickness of this layer is about 156 miles (250 km).
- **Lithosphere:** The solid outer layer of Earth, which is the coolest layer with the least amount of pressure. It includes Earth's crust and a small amount of the upper layer of the mantle. Its thickness varies, but is about 62.5 miles (100 km). This solid layer floats on top of the semisolid athenosphere layer.

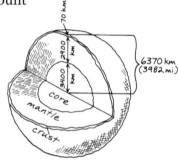

## ACTIVITY: INSIDE OUT

### Purpose

To make a scale model of Earth's three layers based on chemical composition.

### Materials

drawing compass
metric ruler
12-inch (30-cm) square of cardboard
12-inch square of corrugated cardboard
glue
3 apple-size pieces of modeling clay—
   1 each of yellow, red, and blue
1 round toothpick
6-inch (15-cm) piece of string
scissors
6-by-9-inch (15-by-22.5-cm) white, unlined
   index card
fine-tipped black marker

## Procedure

1. Use the compass to draw a 13.6-cm-diameter circle in the center of the cardboard.
2. Draw a second circle around the first one, with a diameter of 25.2 cm. The circumference of this circle will be 5.8 cm from the circumference of the inner circle. Glue this piece of cardboard on top of the corrugated cardboard.
3. Fill the inner circle with yellow clay and the outer circle with red clay.
4. Use the blue clay to make an outline as thin as possible around the circle of red clay.
5. Break the toothpick in half. Discard one piece and stand the other piece in the center of the yellow circle of clay with the pointed end up.
6. Lay the string across the clay model from the edge of the blue clay to the center as shown. Use the scissors to cut off the extra string extending past the blue edge.
7. Use the index card to prepare a stand-up legend. Do this by folding the index card in half with the small sides together. Write the legend on one side of the card, indicating the color name and depth of each layer found in the Earth Layer table. The legend should also include the radius of Earth. Use colored circles to represent the color of each layer and glue a piece of the string to the card to indicate Earth's radius, which is about 3,985.5 miles (6,370 km).

| Earth Layers | | |
|---|---|---|
| **Layer** | | **Depth in Miles (km)** |
| **Color** | **Name** | |
| Yellow | Core | 2,129.5 (3,400) |
| Red | Mantle | 1,812 (2,900) |
| Blue | Crust | 44 (70) |

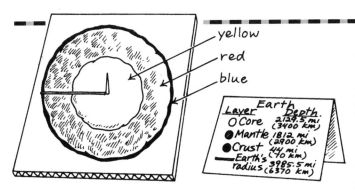

yellow
red
blue

Earth
| Layer | Depth |
|---|---|
| ○ Core | 2124.5 mi (3400 km) |
| ◉ Mantle | 1812 mi (2900 km) |
| ● Crust | 44 mi (70 km) |
| ▬ Earth's radius | 3985.5 mi (6370 km) |

## Results

You have made a scale model of Earth's layers.

## Why?

A **scale model** is a replica made in proportion to the object it represents. A **scale** is a ratio between the measurements of a diagram or model and the actual measurements of an object. In a scale ratio, the drawing or model measurement comes first. If the first value of the ratio is smaller, the scale drawing or model is reduced, as is the case with the 1cm/500 km in this activity. (See Appendix 10 for information on determining a scale.)

The three layers of clay represent the three layers of Earth's interior as separated by their chemical composition. The inner yellow layer represents Earth's core, which is mostly iron. Using a scale of 1 cm equals 500 km (312.5 miles), a diameter of 13.6 cm for the yellow layer represents 6,800 km (4,259 miles), which is the average diameter of Earth's core.

Surrounding the core is the mantle, which is made up of silicates combined with iron and magnesium. This layer has a thickness of about 1,812 miles (2,900 km), so the thickness of the red clay representing this layer is 5.8 cm.

The outer crust of Earth is made mostly of silicates combined with aluminum, iron, and magnesium. This thin outer layer varies from about 5 miles to 44 miles (8 km to 70 km) in thickness. On our scale, that means the blue clay band around the outside representing the crust should be about 0.016 cm to 0.14 cm thick.

The toothpick represents Earth's axis and the string shows Earth's radius, which is about 3,985.5 miles (6,370 km).

## ON YOUR OWN!

To accompany the model of Earth's three chemical layers, prepare a layered book showing Earth divided into five layers based on their physical state (solid, liquid, or in between). See Appendix 2 for instructions for making a six-page layered book. Draw a triangle over the bottom of the book's layers and label

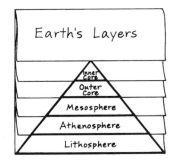

each layer, as shown. Within the triangle, trace along the edges of each layer.

Lift each layer and write a description of the layer represented. Finish the top edge of the triangle if needed. Also include an arc showing a cutaway section of Earth with the diameter of the layer.

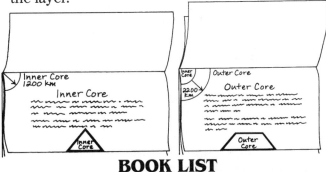

## BOOK LIST

National Wildlife Federation. *Geology: The Active Earth.* New York: Learning Triangle Press, 1997. Information as well as indoor and outdoor activities about Earth, including its inner layers.

James, Ian. *Planet Earth.* Bath, Great Britain: Miles Kelly Publishing Ltd., 1999. More than 100 questions and answers about Earth, including some about the different layers of Earth.

*Planet Earth.* Alexandria, Va.: Time-Life Books, 1997. Information about Earth from past to present, including Earth's layers.

VanCleave, Janice. *Janice VanCleave's Earth Science for Every Kid.* New York: Wiley, 1991. Fun, simple Earth science experiments, including information about Earth's layers.

# Blasters

## *Make a Model of a Volcano!*

A **volcano** is the mountain or hill formed by the accumulation of materials that erupted through one or more openings in Earth's surface. The pipelike openings that connect the volcano's **crater** (depression at the top) to the **magma chamber** (the pool of molten rock deep within Earth) are called **volcanic vents.**

Volcanoes form because of heat and pressure within Earth. When the temperature is high enough, rock melts. This molten rock, called **magma,** has a lower density than the solid rock around it. **Density** is a measure of the mass or weight of a given volume of a material. Being less dense, magma slowly rises toward the surface of Earth. Magma that reaches Earth's surface through vents is called **lava.** A **volcanic eruption** is when lava, ash, debris, and/or gas are thrown out of a volcano. Some eruptions are very explosive, while others are relatively quiet outpourings of lava or gas.

Some volcanoes on Earth are **active** (erupted within the last century), but most of them are **dormant** (inactive). Dormant volcanoes have not erupted in hundreds of years, but they could. Volcanoes that have not erupted in thousands of years are considered **extinct** and most likely will never again become active. There are more than 5,000 active underwater volcanoes and more than 800 active above-sea volcanoes currently in existence around the world.

Different types of eruptions produce different kinds of volcanoes. Explosive eruptions throw lava high into the air. The lava cools and hardens into a different volcanic material called **tephra** (lava blasted into the air by a violent volcanic eruption that solidifies as it falls to the ground). Tephra comes in different sizes, including ash, cinders, and large rocks called **volcanic bombs.** A **cinder cone volcano** is formed by an explosive eruption in which tephra piles up into a steep-sided, loosely packed cone. As the tephra falls back down around the vent, the heavier materials fall near the vent and the lighter-weight materials are thrown farther away. This type of volcano usually has a rounded top with a small bowl-shaped crater. The upper parts of the volcano are steep with a more gently sloping base. There are many cinder cone volcanoes in the western United States, such as Sunset Crater in Arizona. These volcanoes are also found in many other parts of Earth, including the island of Java, in Indonesia.

A **shield volcano** (a volcano composed of layers of solidified lava, a wide base, and a large, bowl-shaped opening—crater—at the top) is generally less steep and shorter than other types of volcanoes. It is made by repeated eruptions producing lava flows. The lava forming this volcano is relatively thin and flows away from the vent. As the lava cools, it becomes thicker, flows more slowly, and finally becomes solid. Mauna Loa in Hawaii is one of the largest shield volcanoes in the world (and also the world's largest active volcano). Its top is 13,677 feet (4,103 m) above sea level and 28,000 feet (8,400 m) above its base, which rests on the ocean floor.

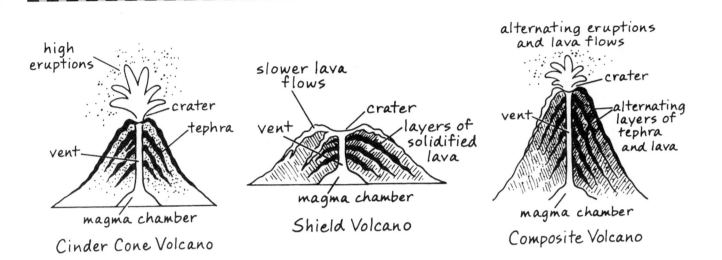

high eruptions
crater
tephra
vent
magma chamber
**Cinder Cone Volcano**

slower lava flows
crater
vent
layers of solidified lava
magma chamber
**Shield Volcano**

alternating eruptions and lava flows
crater
vent
alternating layers of tephra and lava
magma chamber
**Composite Volcano**

A **composite volcano** (a cone-shaped volcano formed by alternating layers of solidified lava and rock particles) is a combination of a cinder cone and a shield volcano that results from alternating eruptions of volcanic debris and lava. This type of volcano is likely to be the tallest and steepest volcano. Mount Rainier, in the state of Washington, is an example of a composite volcano.

## ACTIVITY: BUBBLER

### Purpose

To make a model of an erupting volcano.

### Materials

ruler
scissors
string
pencil
2 poster boards at least 17 inches (42.5 cm) square
8-ounce (240-mL) empty plastic bottle
masking tape
round tray with diameter of at least 16 inches (40 cm)

2 cups (500 mL) plaster of Paris
3-cup (750-mL) plastic throwaway container
1-cup (250-mL) measuring cup
tap water
wooden craft stick
liquid tempera paints—brown, black, red
art brush
2 tablespoons (30 mL) liquid dishwashing soap
red food coloring
effervescent tablet, such as Alka-Seltzer

### Procedure

1. Draw a circle on each poster board, one with an 8-inch (20-cm) radius and the other with a radius of 7 inches (17.5 cm). (See Appendix 11 for instructions on drawing large circles.) Call the larger circle A and the smaller one B.

2. Cut out the circles.

3. On circle A, use the pencil to draw a circle that is about the size of a quarter in the center of the paper. Cut out the circle by cutting from one edge of the paper, along a radius, then around the drawn circle.

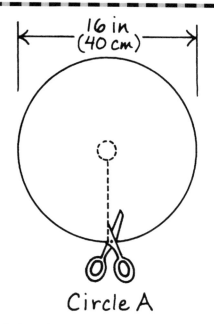

**16 in (40 cm)**

Circle A

4. Stand the plastic bottle in the center of paper circle B. Tape the bottle to the paper.

5. Overlap the cut edges of paper circle A to form a cone with a large and a small open end. Stand the cone over the plastic bottle and adjust the amount the edges overlap so that the cone's height is equal to that of the bottle. The mouth of the bottle should be at or near the small open end of the cone. Secure the overlapped edges of the cone with tape.

6. Use tape to secure the mouth of the bottle to the small hole in the cone.

7. With the cone centered on paper circle B, secure the edges of the cone to the paper circle with tape. You have made the foundation for a volcano.

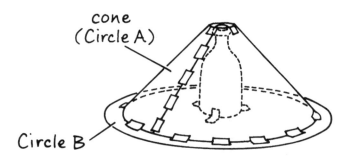

cone (Circle A)

Circle B

8. Place the volcano foundation in the tray.

9. Prepare the plaster of Paris using these steps:

   a. Pour the plaster in the plastic container.

   b. Add 1 cup of water to the container of plaster.

   c. Use the wooden stick to mix the plaster and the water.

10. Using the wooden stick, spread the wet plaster of Paris over the outside surface of the cone and exposed area of paper circle B. Make the surface as rough as possible. Allow the plaster to dry, which will take 20 to 30 minutes.

11. Use the brown and black paint to color the volcano. Paint a red stripe down one side to represent a lava flow.

red "lava"

12. Model an eruption of the volcano by pouring ¾ cup (188 mL) of water into the bottle inside the volcano.

13. Add the liquid dishwashing soap to the bottle.

14. Add 10 or more drops of red food coloring to the bottle.

15. Break the effervescent tablet into four or more pieces that will fit into the opening of the volcano. Add two to three tablet pieces to the bottle. Add more pieces when the foaming slows or stops.

## Results

You have made a model of an erupting volcano.

## Why?

The effervescent tablet pieces react with water, producing a gas, carbon dioxide. This gas creates bubbles in the soapy water that rise in the bottle, and red foam representing lava flows down the side of the volcano model.

## ON YOUR OWN

The parts of a volcano can be displayed on a backboard. (See Appendix 1 for more on making a three-paneled backboard.) Draw a colored cross-section of a composite volcano on the center panel of a three-paneled backboard, with the volcano's base extending to the side panels. The right and left panels of the backboard can be used to label and define the parts of the volcano, as shown. The model of the volcano can be placed in front of the backboard.

## BOOK LIST

Farndon, John. *How the Earth Works.* Pleasantville, N.Y.: Reader's Digest, 1992. Investigations that let you discover the answers to questions about Earth, including some about volcanoes.

National Wildlife Federation. *Geology: The Active Earth.* New York: Learning Triangle, 1997. Information as well as indoor and outdoor activities about volcanoes and other geology topics.

VanCleave, Janice. *Janice VanCleave's Volcanoes.* New York: Wiley, 1994. Experiments about volcanic eruptions and other volcano topics. Each chapter contains ideas that can be turned into award-winning science fair projects.

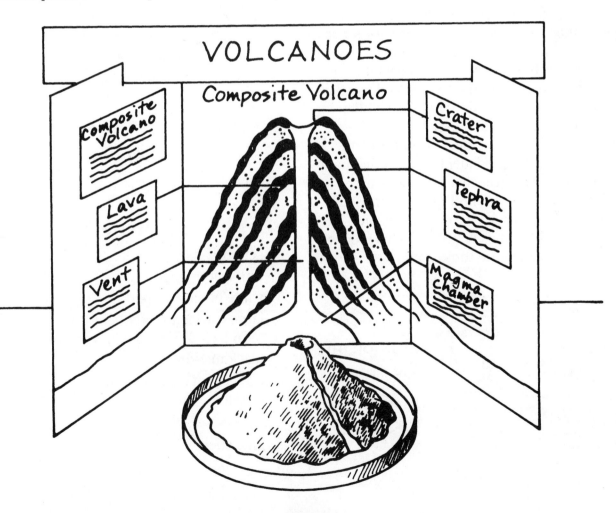

# Rock from Rock

*Make a Model of the Rock Cycle!*

A **rock** is a naturally occurring solid made up of one or more minerals. A **mineral** is a substance made of a single kind of element or chemical compound with these four basic characteristics: (1) it occurs naturally; (2) it is **inorganic** (a substance that is not alive, never was alive, and was not made by life processes); (3) it has a definite chemical composition; and (4) it is a crystalline solid.

The three basic types of rock are igneous, sedimentary, and metamorphic. **Igneous rock** is formed by the cooling and solidifying of liquid rock. **Sedimentary rock** is formed from deposits of **sediment** (loose rock and soil that have been carried by wind, rain, or ice) that are **compacted** (packed together) and **cemented** (stuck together). **Metamorphic rock** is igneous or sedimentary rock that has been changed by great heat and pressure within Earth's crust. Through different processes, each rock type can be changed into one of the other types in the trio. This process of change is called the **rock cycle.**

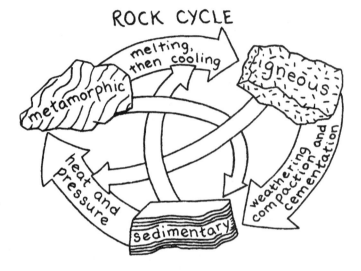

## ACTIVITY: NEVER ENDING

### Purpose

To model the rock cycle.

### Materials

scissors
transparent tape
white butcher paper
large cardboard box (a box with two 18-by-26-inch (45-by-65-cm) sides works well)
black marker
3 sheets of colored copy paper
pencil
ruler
glue stick

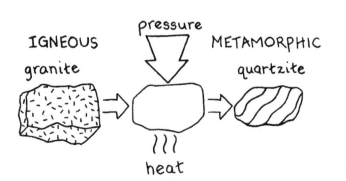

## Procedure

1. Using the scissors and tape, wrap the box with the butcher paper so that one of the larger sides has a smooth covering.

2. Use the marker to write the title "Rock Cycle" on one of the long edges of the large, smooth-covered side of the box.

3. Use one of the sheets of copy paper to make a large tab book. (See Appendix 3, Part B for instructions on how to make a large tab book.)

4. Write information about sedimentary rock formation on the inside of the tab book.

5. On the outside of the tab book, draw a diagram representing sedimentary rock or use a picture of a sedimentary rock. Label the tab book "Sedimentary Rock."

6. Repeat steps 3 through 5 two times, making a tab book for igneous rock and another for metamorphic rock.

7. Turn the box so that the smooth-covered side faces up.

8. Place the tab books on the box as shown, with "Sedimentary Rock" beneath the title. With the pencil, lightly trace around the tab books on the poster board. Remove the tab books from the poster board and keep them for step 10.

9. Use the ruler to draw arrows on the poster board between the outlines of each of the tab books, extending the lines into the traced space for the tab books, as shown. Add the information as shown on the diagram within each arrow.

10. Use the glue to attach the tab books to the box. Stand the box so the tab books face out.

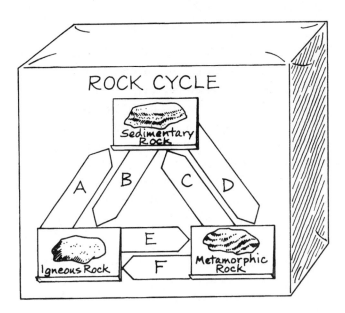

## Results

You have made a model of the rock cycle.

## Why?

Rocks come from other rocks. Igneous rock forms when sedimentary or metamorphic rock melts, cools, and solidifies. **Weathering** (the process by which rocks are broken into smaller pieces) of igneous and metamorphic rocks produces sediment, which forms sedimentary rock. Metamorphic rock forms when igneous or sedimentary rock is changed in structure, appearance, and composition by temperature and pressure within Earth's crust.

The rock cycle model made in this activity places sedimentary rocks at the top of the model. This is because sedimentary rocks are formed when the other rocks are lifted to or are near the top of Earth's surface, while the formation of metamorphic and igneous rocks occurs generally below Earth's surface.

## ON YOUR OWN!

In front of the rock cycle model, display rock samples representing the three types of rocks and a legend for each rock type. The different types of rocks can be displayed in egg cartons with a title of the rock type inside the lid. A binder divided into three sections for each rock type can be prepared and displayed with the samples. An information sheet for each rock sample should be in the binder.

Label each rock sample by using the following steps:

1. Use the brush from a bottle of liquid paper to paint a small spot of liquid paper on each rock sample. Place the spot in an unimportant area of the rock. A different color of liquid paper can be used for each of the rock types.

2. When the liquid paper has dried, use a black fine-point permanent pen to write a reference number on each spot.

## BOOK LIST

O'Donoghue, Michael. *Rocks & Minerals of the World.* San Diego: Thunder Bay Press, 1994. Information, including colored photographs and experiments, about rocks and minerals.

VanCleave, Janice. *Janice VanCleave's Rocks and Minerals.* New York: Wiley, 1996. Experiments about types of rocks and other rock and mineral topics. Each chapter contains ideas that can be turned into award-winning science fair projects.

# Slipping

## *Make a Model of Faults!*

**Stress** (force) can cause rocks to **fracture** (to break with rough or jagged edges). If there is no movement along the fracture, the fracture is called a **joint.** If there is movement, the fracture is called a **fault.** The fracture line of a fault is called the **fault plane.** If the fault plane shows vertical motion, the **fault block** (the rock on either side of a fault plane) above the fault plane is called the **hanging wall** and the fault block below the fault plane is called the **footwall.** Fault types are classified by how one side of a fault is pushed out of place in a given direction relative to the other side.

The three basic types of stress acting on Earth's crust are tension, compression, and shearing. **Tension** is a stretching force that can be strong enough to pull rocks apart. **Compression** is a squeezing force that pushes rocks together, causing them to **rumple** (crush into wrinkles), fold, and sometimes break. **Shear** is a force that pushes on rock from different directions, causing it to twist and break. When the stress on the crust is from tension, the hanging wall of the fault moves down in relationship to the footwall. This is called a **normal fault.**

Compression causes a **reverse fault.** This fault is similar to a normal fault, except the hanging wall moves upward in relation to the footwall. Normal and reverse faults are also called **dip-slip faults** because their movement is vertical. The fault plane is usually at a slant.

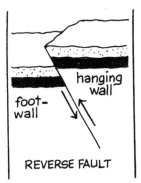

REVERSE FAULT

Shearing produces a **lateral fault,** also called a **strike-slip fault.** The movement of the fault blocks along a vertical fault plane are mainly horizontal, to the left or right, with little to no up-and-down movement. Left or right direction is determined by an observer standing on either fault block; the movement of the other block is a **left lateral fault** if it is to the left, or a **right lateral fault** if it is to the right of the observer.

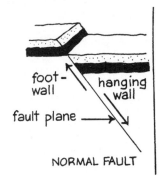

NORMAL FAULT

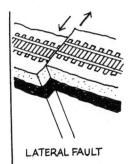

LATERAL FAULT

Faults can be only a few inches (cm) or many thousands of miles (km) long. The San Andreas Fault along the western part of North America is at least 812 miles (1,300 km) long. It is mostly made up of many right lateral faults that are parallel to each other. In the last two million years, Earth's crust along this fault has moved about 10 miles (16 km). Movement along faults is what causes **earthquakes** (shaking of the ground caused by rapid movement of Earth's crust).

## ACTIVITY: NORMAL FAULT

### Purpose

To make a model of a normal fault.

### Materials

two lemon-size pieces of clay of different colors
table knife
2 round toothpicks
8-by-8-inch (20-by-20-cm) square piece of poster board
marker

### Procedure

1. Break each piece of clay in half.

2. Shape each piece of clay into a roll about 4 inches (10 cm) long.

3. Lay the clay rolls together, one on top of the other, alternating the colors.

4. Press the rolls together into one large clay piece. Flatten the sides of the clay piece by tapping them against a hard surface, such as a table.

5. Use the table knife to cut the clay pieces into two parts diagonally.

6. Secure the layers in each section together by inserting one toothpick through the layers, top to bottom.

7. Lay the sections together on the square piece of poster board so that the colored layers match up, then move the left section of the clay layers up and the right section down, as shown.

8. Label the poster board with the names of the fault parts and with the title "Normal Fault."

### Results

You have made a model of a normal fault.

### Why?

The clay is cut and shifted so that the layers of colored clay in the two sections no longer form a continuous horizontal line. Each clay color represents a layer of one kind of rock material. Cutting the clay represents the stress that causes rocks to fracture. Moving the broken pieces represents a fault.

While the hanging wall and footwall of the model both moved, it is not always possible to determine whether the fault blocks of Earth's crust both move or one stands still while the other moves past it. Since the model shows the hanging wall lower than the footwall, the model represents a normal fault.

## ON YOUR OWN!

1. Repeat the original experiment twice to make two more clay models, one to represent a reverse fault and one to represent a lateral fault. Display the models for each type of fault. For each model, prepare an information card on a 6-by-8-inch (15-by-20-cm) index card that includes a drawing with labels of the different parts of the fault being represented. Use a circle stand to support the information cards. (See Appendix 12 for instructions on making a circle stand.)

2. You can also make and display paper models for normal and reverse faults. Make these models by cutting strips of colored construction paper of varying widths and gluing them lengthwise on a sheet of white construction paper. Leave spaces between some of the strips so that the white paper shows through. Allow the glue to dry, then cut the paper in two parts diagonally, as shown.

Move the hanging wall down for a normal fault. Use tape on the back of the pieces to secure them in this position. Repeat, making a second sheet, but move the hanging wall upward to indicate a reverse fault.

## BOOK LIST

Farndon, John. *How the Earth Works.* Pleasantville, N.Y.: Reader's Digest, 1992. Investigations, including some about faults, that let you discover the answers to questions about Earth.

James, Ian. *Planet Earth.* Bath, Great Britain: Miles Kelly Publishing Ltd., 1999. More than a hundred questions and answers about Earth, including some about faults.

Parsons, Alexandra. *Make It Work! Earth.* Ocala, Fla.: Action Publishing, 1992. Models and information about Earth, including deformation by fracturing.

Ruiz, Andres Llamas, et al. *Volcanos and Earthquakes.* New York: Sterling Publishing, 1997. Information about the causes of faults and the relationships between faults, earthquakes, and volcanoes.

VanCleave, Janice. *Janice VanCleave's Earthquakes.* New York: Wiley, 1993. Experiments about faults and other earthquake-related topics. Each chapter contains ideas that can be turned into award-winning science fair projects.

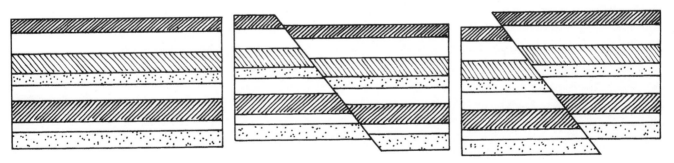

NORMAL FAULT     REVERSE FAULT

# V

# PHYSICS

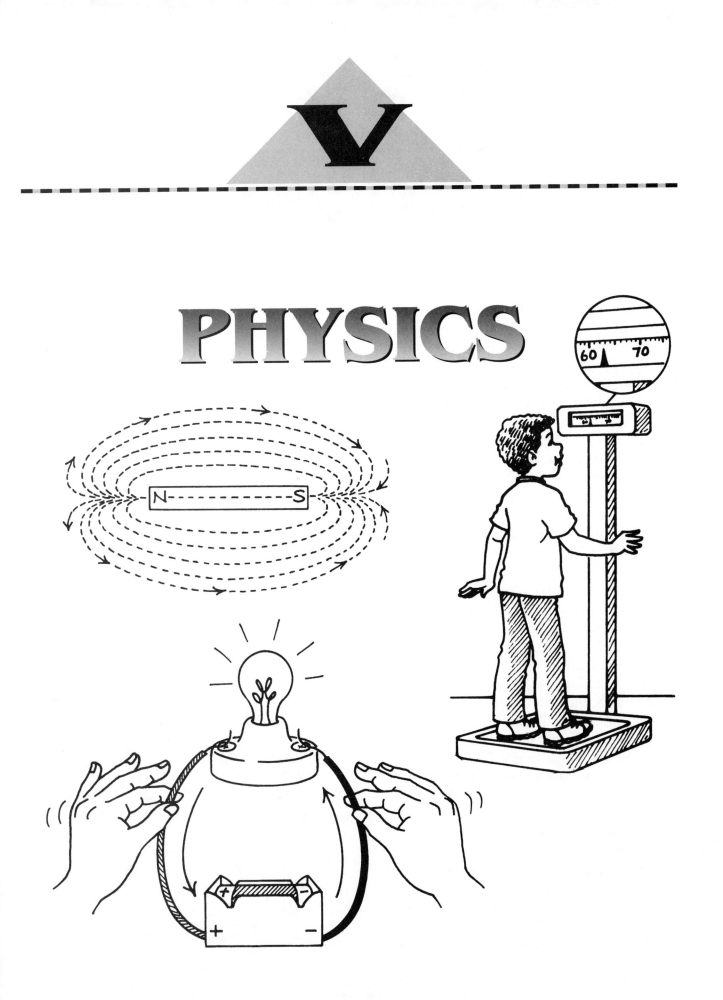

# Weighty

## Make a Model of Gravity!

Gravity is the force of attraction between objects due to their mass. The more massive an object is, the greater is its gravity. Earth attracts objects of lesser mass with a gravitational force that causes the objects to **accelerate** (increase in speed) toward Earth at a rate commonly referred to as one *g,* or one Earth gravity. This acceleration due to gravity is called **gravitational acceleration.** The gravitational acceleration for Earth is about 32 ft/sec$^2$ (9.8 m/sec$^2$), which means that, if the resistance due to air is not considered, the speed of a falling object increases at a rate of about 32 ft/ sec (9.8 m/sec) each second the object falls. (**Air** is the name of the mixture of gases in Earth's atmosphere.)

Thus, not considering air resistance, a rock dropped from the Tower of Pisa, which is 180 feet (54 m) high, would have a speed of about 107.2 ft/sec (32.2 m/sec), which is equal to 73 miles/hr (117 km/hr) when it hit the ground.

On Earth, the weight of an object is the measure of the gravitational force exerted on it by Earth. The weight of an object can be determined with this equation: $F_{wt} = m \times g,$ which is read as force weight ($F_{wt}$) equals mass ($m$) times gravitational acceleration ($g$). Since Earth's gravitational acceleration is relatively constant, as the mass of an object increases, the object's weight, which is the force of gravity acting on it, increases. This means that an object with more mass has more weight, and thus has a greater gravitational force acting on it. Gravitational acceleration ($g$) can be expressed as a ratio of force weight per mass:

$g = F_{wt}/m$. The ratio of the force weight of an object and the mass of the object always equals about 32 ft/sec$^2$ (9.8 m/sec$^2$) on Earth. Therefore, no matter how heavy or light an object is, if gravity is the only force acting on an object, it falls at a gravitational acceleration of 32 ft/sec$^2$ (9.8 m/sec$^2$).

Since mass is a measure of the amount of matter in an object, as the mass of an object increases so does its weight. A **spring scale,** such as a bathroom scale, is an instrument that measures the weight of an object. The spring scale records a different weight for different masses, so as you grow your weight increases, which means that you have had an increase in mass. If, however, you used the spring scale on a planet with a different gravitational pull than Earth, it would record different weights for the same masses measured on Earth.

## ACTIVITY: SPRING SCALE

### Purpose

To model how a spring scale measures gravity (weight).

### Materials

2 large paper clips
4-by-6-inch (10-by-15-cm) piece of corrugated cardboard
scissors
rubber band
ruler
drinking straw
pen
3-ounce (90-mL) paper cup
12-inch (30-cm) piece of string
narrow three-paneled backboard (see Appendix 1)
marker
⅜-by-36-inch (0.94-by-90-cm) dowel
transparent tape
two 6-by-9-inch (15-by-22.5-cm) unlined white index cards
lemon-size piece of clay

### Procedure

1. Attach one of the paper clips to one of the short sides of the cardboard at the center. This will be paper clip A.

2. Cut the rubber band to form one long strip.

3. Tie one end of the rubber band to the end of paper clip A.

4. Cut a 2-inch (5-cm) piece from the straw.

5. Thread the rubber band through the short piece of straw. Secure the straw to the cardboard so that it is just below paper clip A.

6. Tie the free end of the rubber band to the second paper clip, which will be paper clip B.

7. Lay the cardboard on a flat surface and pull the rubber band straight without stretching it. Make a mark on the cardboard at the top of paper clip B. Draw a horizontal line across the cardboard at this mark.

8. Make 10 additional marks below this line every 0.5 cm.

9. Starting at the top line, number the lines 0 through 10.

10. With the pen, make holes on opposite sides of the cup beneath its rim.

11. Tie the ends of the string in the holes in the cup, forming a loop.

12. Attach the loop to paper clip B.

13. Prepare a narrow three-paneled backboard, using the instructions in Appendix 1. Use the marker to print a title at the top of the center panel, such as "Weight vs. Mass."

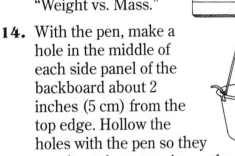

14. With the pen, make a hole in the middle of each side panel of the backboard about 2 inches (5 cm) from the top edge. Hollow the holes with the pen so they are about the same size as the dowel. Ask an adult to cut off any excess dowel length.

15. Push the dowel through the holes in the backboard.

16. Secure the top of the piece of cardboard to the center of the dowel with tape. The cardboard should be centered in front of the backboard's center panel.

**17.** Using the pen, title one of the index cards "Weight," then write information about weight on the card, including how weight and gravity compare. Use tape to secure the card to the bottom left side of the center panel of the display.

**18.** Using the pen, title the other index card "Mass," then write information about mass on the card. Use tape to secure the card to the bottom right side of the center panel of the display.

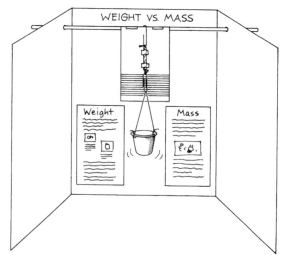

**19.** Divide the clay by pulling off a grape-size piece.

**20.** Use the spring scale model to demonstrate the difference in weight of objects with different masses. Do this by placing the small piece of clay in the cup and noting the line closest to the top of paper clip B. Repeat, using the larger piece of clay.

## Results

You have made a spring scale model that shows how weight is measured.

## Why?

The spring scale model demonstrates that as mass in the cup increases, the cup is pulled down with a greater force. This downward force is Earth's gravity acting on the cup. The greater the mass of the object, the greater the downward movement, and thus the greater the gravitational force on the object. Since the weight of an object is the measure of the gravitational force acting on it, the model demonstrates that as the mass of an object increases, the weight of the object increases. While the model does not accurately measure weight, it can be used to make a comparison of objects with different weights.

## ON YOUR OWN!

An object on Earth would have the same mass but a different weight than that same object on the Moon. This is because the Moon has a lower gravitational acceleration than Earth. Since mass is the amount of matter in an object, a change in the value of gravitational acceleration changes an object's weight but doesn't change its mass. The **gravity rate (GR)** of a celestial body is its gravitational acceleration divided by Earth's gravitational acceleration. So, Earth's GR equals 32 ft/sec$^2$ ÷ 32 ft/sec$^2$ = 1 (9.8 m/sec$^2$ ÷ 9.8 m/sec$^2$ = 1). Celestial bodies with a gravity rate greater than 1 have a gravitational acceleration greater than that of Earth. Those with a gravity rate less than 1 have a gravitational acceleration less than that of Earth. Your weight measured in pounds on each planet can be calculated using these steps:

**1.** Determine your weight in pounds on Earth by weighing yourself on a scale.

**2.** Use a calculator to multiply your weight on Earth in pounds by the gravity rate of each planet and Earth's Moon, as listed in the "Weight Data" table. For example, if you weigh 90 pounds on Earth, your weight on Earth's Moon, which has a gravity rate of 0.17, would be:

90 pounds × 0.17 = 15.3 pounds

A table showing your weight on different planets and the Moon can be displayed on one of the side panels of the backboard. On the remaining side panel, you can display a diagram, like the one shown here, indicating your mass and weight on Earth and your mass and weight on the Moon and/or another planet. Your weight in pounds and the ratio 1 kg/2.2 pounds can be used to determine your mass. For example, if you weigh 90 pounds on Earth, multiply your weight by 1 kg/2.2 pounds to determine your mass in kilograms.

90 pounds × 1 kg/2.2 pounds = 41 kg

Note: If you wish to measure your weight in the metric unit of **newtons,** multiply your weight in pounds times the multiple 4.5 N/1 lb.

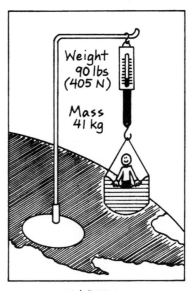

EARTH

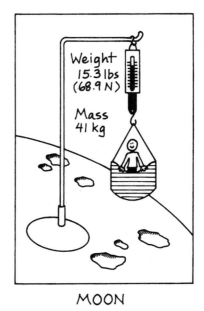

MOON

| Weight Data | |
|---|---|
| **Planet** | **Gravity Rate (G.R.)** |
| Mercury | 0.38 |
| Venus | 0.91 |
| Earth | 1.00 |
| Mars | 0.38 |
| Jupiter | 2.54 |
| Saturn | 1.16 |
| Uranus | 0.91 |
| Neptune | 1.19 |
| Pluto | 0.06 |
| Earth's Moon | 0.17 |

## BOOK LIST

Couper, Heather, and Nigel Henbest. *How the Universe Works.* Pleasantville, N.Y.: Reader's Digest, 1994. Interesting facts and activities about gravity and other astronomy topics.

Filkin, David. *Stephen Hawking's Universe: The Cosmos Explained.* New York: Basic Books, 1997. A brief history of the cosmos, including information about gravity.

Gilbert, Harry, and Diana Gilbert Smith. *Gravity, the Glue of the Universe.* Englewood, Colo.: Teacher Ideas Press, 1997. Information and activities about gravity.

VanCleave, Janice. *Janice VanCleave's Gravity.* New York: Wiley, 1993. Fun facts and investigations about gravity.

# Movers

*Make a Model of Mechanical Energy!*

**Energy** is the ability of an object to cause changes. It is also defined as the ability to do **work** (what is accomplished when a force causes an object to move). It was while thinking about why objects move that scientists first began to develop the idea of energy. In 1583 at the age of 19, the Italian scientist Galileo Galilei (1564–1642) observed that a swinging church lamp swung upward very nearly as high as the point from which it had previously swung downward. He used his pulse to time the swinging lamp and discovered that the time of the upswing was equal to that of the downswing. Galileo couldn't explain why the lamp swung back and forth, but his observations laid the groundwork for future scientists who further experimented and explained the types of energy involved in the movement of a swinging lamp.

In 1807, Thomas Young, an English physicist (1773–1829), was the first to use the word energy. He defined energy as the ability to do work. Work is the amount of force on an object times the distance the object moves in the direction of the force. The first form of energy as defined by Young was **mechanical energy** (the energy of motion). It is the energy of an object that is moving or is capable of motion. Today, physicists generally think of mechanical energy as being the sum of the **kinetic energy, KE** (energy that a moving object has because of its motion) and **potential energy, PE** (energy of position or condition of an object). Kinetic energy can be changed into potential energy or vice versa. In the diagram,

in position A, the swing is at its highest position and is not moving, thus it has maximum potential energy, PE, and zero kinetic energy, KE. As the swing starts to move toward position B, its PE changes to KE. So at position B, all of its PE has been changed to KE. As the swing moves toward position C, its kinetic energy begins to change to potential energy again, until at position C it has maximum PE and zero KE, and so on.

The term *kinetic energy* comes from the Greek word *kinema*, for "motion" (which also inspired the modern term *cinema*). When a ball rolls down a hill, it has kinetic energy

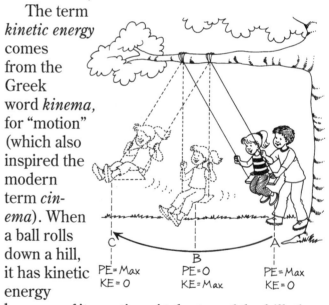

PE=Max    PE=0    PE=Max
KE=0      KE=Max  KE=0

because of its motion. At the top of the hill, the ball has mechanical energy stored up in it because of its position on the hill. This stored mechanical energy is called **gravitational potential energy, GPE** (potential energy due to the height of an object above a surface). At the top of the hill the ball has maximum GPE and zero KE. Because of gravity the ball rolls down the hill. As the ball rolls, its gravitational potential energy changes to kinetic energy. When the ball is halfway down the hill, half of its GPE has changed to KE, so its GPE equals its KE. At the bottom of the hill, the ball has zero GPE and maximum KE. The change of energy from one form to another is called **energy conversion.**

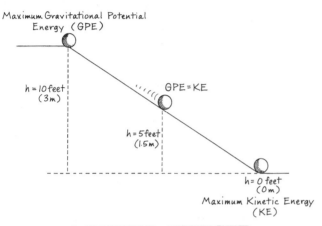

## ACTIVITY: SWINGER

### Purpose

To model the energy conversions of a swinging pendulum.

### Materials

paper hole punch

10-by-12-inch (25-by-30-cm) piece of yellow
   poster board (any pale color will work)

fine-point black marker

ruler

three 12-inch (30-cm) pieces of string

three metal washers

glue

transparent tape

### Procedure

**1.** Use the paper hole punch to cut a hole in the middle and about 1 inch (2.5 cm) from the edge of one of the short sides of the poster board.

**2.** Use the marker and the ruler to draw three lines of equal length and no longer than 8 inches (20 cm), starting at the same point at the bottom of the hole in the poster board. One line should be straight down the poster board and the other two lines should be diagonal from the hole toward the corners of the poster board, as shown.

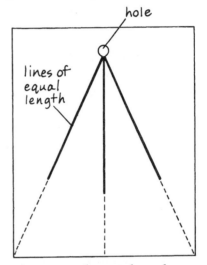

**3.** Tie a string to each metal washer.

**4.** Glue a washer to the end of each line on the poster board. Allow the glue to dry.

**5.** Push the free end of one of the strings through the hole in the poster board. Pull the string taut so that it lies flat along the black line drawn from the washer to the hole. Tape the end of the string to the back of the poster board.

**6.** Repeat step 5, using the strings tied to the remaining washers.

**7.** Using the marker, add these labels to the poster board:

- a title, such as "Energy Conversion"

- dashed lines and arrows showing the motion of the pendulum

- the relationship of potential energy (PE) and kinetic energy (KE), as shown in the diagram

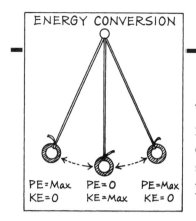

ENERGY CONVERSION

PE=Max    PE=0      PE=Max
KE=0      KE=Max    KE=0

## Results

You have made a model of the energy conversions of a swinging pendulum.

## Why?

A **pendulum** is a weight hung so that it is free to swing about a fixed point. When a pendulum swings back and forth, energy is continually changed from gravitational potential to kinetic energy. The change of energy from one form to another is called energy conversion. When anything falls, energy is converted from potential to kinetic. At the end of each swing, the pendulum stops and reverses direction. At the end of the swing, the pendulum is at its highest position and has only gravitational potential energy (GPE) and no kinetic energy (KE). As gravity pulls on the pendulum it swings down, and its GPE continuously changes to KE. So, at the bottom of the swing, the pendulum has only KE and no GPE. As the pendulum rises, the KE continuously changes to GPE, and so on. The pendulum loses energy due to friction between the pendulum and air, so its height decreases with each swing until it finally stops.

## ON YOUR OWN!

Display the energy conversion model on the center panel of a narrow three-paneled backboard. (For instructions on making the backboard, see Appendix 1, Part A.) Print the title "Mechanical Energy: PE + KE" on the title strip.

On the left panel of the backboard, attach a diagram and information on potential energy drawn on a 6-by-12-inch (15-by-30-cm) piece of poster board. (Note: Use the same color poster board as you used for the energy conversion model.) Include a title, "Potential Energy (PE)," and beneath the title draw a diagram

representing an object with potential energy, such as a large rock on the edge of a high cliff. Beneath the diagram, add information about potential energy, including the definition and examples. Attach this piece of poster board to the left panel of the backboard.

Put information and a diagram about kinetic energy on another 6-by-12-inch (15-by-30-cm) piece of poster board the same color as the other poster board. Include a title, "Kinetic Energy (KE)," and beneath the title draw a diagram representing an object with kinetic energy, such as a moving car. Beneath the diagram, add information about kinetic energy, including the definition and examples. Attach this piece of poster board to the right panel of the backboard.

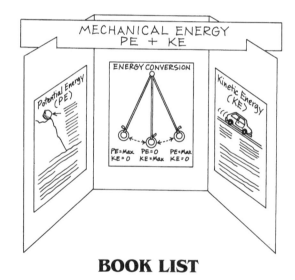

## BOOK LIST

Churchill, E. Richard, et al. *365 More Simple Science Experiments with Everyday Materials.* New York: Black Dog & Leventhal Publishers, Inc., 1998. Simple experiments, including some about pendulums.

Doherty, Paul, and Don Rathjen. *The Spinning Blackboard and Other Dynamic Experiments on Force and Motion.* New York: Wiley, 1996. Experiments about force and motion, including some about pendulums.

Suplee, Curt. *Everyday Science Explained.* Washington, D.C.: National Geographic Society, 1998. Science information that encourages readers to explore everyday life, including facts about energy conversions.

VanCleave, Janice. *Janice VanCleave's Physics for Every Kid.* New York: Wiley, 1991. Fun, simple physics experiments, including information about pendulums.

# 23

# Pathways

## *Make a Model of Electric Circuits!*

The property of particles within atoms that causes the particles to attract or repel one another is called a **charge.** There are two known types of charges: positive and negative. A **proton,** found in the **nucleus** (center) of an atom, has a positive charge of +1. **Electrons,** spinning around the outside of the nucleus, have a negative charge of –1. **Electricity** is a form of energy associated with the presence and movement of electric charges. The buildup of stationary charges is called **static electricity** and the movement of charges is called **current electricity.**

A **battery** is a device that uses chemicals to produce electricity. The ends of the battery are called **terminals** (the points at which connections are made to an electrical device); one is a **positive terminal** (the terminal with a positive charge) and the other is a **negative terminal** (the terminal with a negative charge). The electrical energy in the battery cannot be used until its two terminals are connected by a **conductor** (a material that easily allows electric charges to pass through it), such as a metal wire. The path through which electric charges move is called an **electric circuit.**

When there is only one path for the electric current to follow, the electric circuit is called a **series circuit.** The arrows in the diagram represent the flow of electricity in a series circuit away from the negative terminal of the battery, through the bulb, and back to the positive terminal of the battery.

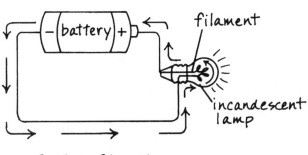

Series Circuit

A **parallel circuit** is an electric circuit in which the electric current has more than one path to follow. The advantage is that, like when you add another lane on a busy freeway, more traffic can flow. With a parallel circuit, more electric current can flow.

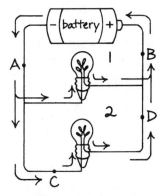

Parallel Circuit

If any part of a series circuit is broken, meaning there is a break in the path formed by the conductors, no current can flow through any part of the circuit and the circuit is said to be an **open circuit.** An electric circuit in the path that is not broken is called a **closed circuit.** In the diagram, if the circuit is broken at points A or B, no current can flow through any part of the circuit. But if the circuit is broken at points C or D, no circuit would flow through lamp 2, but current would flow through lamp 1.

## ACTIVITY: OPEN AND CLOSED

### Purpose

To model a series circuit.

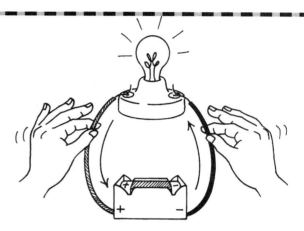

### Materials

1.5-volt size D battery
D-size battery holder with insulated wires (red and black)
flashlight lamp (for E-10 screw-base holder)
lamp holder with E-10 screw-base
wide three-paneled backboard (see Appendix 1, Part B)
(The first four items can be purchased at an electronics store, such as RadioShack.)

### Procedure

1. Place the battery in the battery holder so the battery's negative terminal is at the end with the battery holder's black wire.

2. Screw the lamp into the lamp holder.

3. Holding the insulated part of the wires attached to the battery holder, touch the bare ends of the wires to the screws on either side of the lamp holder. *CAUTION: Do not leave the wires on the screws for more than a few seconds. The bare wire and lamp can get hot enough to burn you. Allow them to cool before touching them.*

4. Observe the lamp when only one wire leading from the negative terminal of the battery touches a screw on the lamp holder.

5. Repeat step 4, using only the wire from the positive terminal.

6. Prepare a backboard by following the instructions in Appendix 1, Part B. Place the series model in front of the backboard. *CAUTION: For safety, place a mock battery such as a paper tube labeled "battery" into the battery holder. This prevents others from connecting the circuit without your supervision. You can place a real battery in the holder if you wish to demonstrate the model.*

7. Create an information sheet about series circuits and secure it to the center panel behind the series circuit model. The information sheet can include an example of a schematic diagram of a series circuit, such as the one shown, as well as an explanation of how current flows through a series circuit.

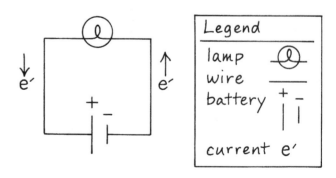

### Results

You have made a model of a series circuit.

## Why?

When the two wires touch either side of the lamp holder, the electric circuit formed by the lamp, the lamp holder, the wire, the battery holder, and the battery is a continuous path called a closed circuit. The light glows when there is a closed circuit. The glow is produced when the **filament** (the small wire inside the bulb) gets hot enough to produce light. When only one of the wires touches the lamp holder, there is a separation of the conducting materials forming the electric circuit, so an open circuit is formed and the light does not glow.

## ON YOUR OWN!

Using two sheets of paper, prepare information sheets about open and closed circuits and parallel circuits, including definitions, diagrams, and/or pictures representing them. Schematic diagrams can be used. Title the display "Electric Pathways."

## BOOK LIST

Gundersen, P. Erik. *The Handy Physics Answer Book.* Detroit: Visible Ink, 1999. Interesting information about physics topics, including some about electric currents.

VanCleave, Janice. *Janice VanCleave's Electricity.* New York: Wiley, 1994. A collection of fun experiments about electricity.

# Attractive

## *Make a Model of Magnetism!*

A **magnet** is an object that attracts iron and other magnetic materials, including cobalt and nickel. The attraction that magnets have for each other or for magnetic materials is called **magnetic force** or **magnetism.** The space around a magnet in which it can affect magnetic material and/or another magnet is called its **magnetic field.**

Magnets and magnetic materials contain **domains** (groups of atoms that act like tiny magnets). When a magnetic material is placed near a magnet, the domains in the material line up in the direction of the magnet's magnetic field. This causes the material to be temporarily magnetized. Generally, when the material is removed from the magnetic field, the domains move back to a disorderly arrangement within a short period of time. While all magnets are made of magnetic materials, all magnetic materials are not magnetized. For example, an iron nail is a magnetic material. When iron is magnetized, many of the domains are lined up so that they face in the same direction. If iron is not magnetized material, the domains in the iron face in many different directions.

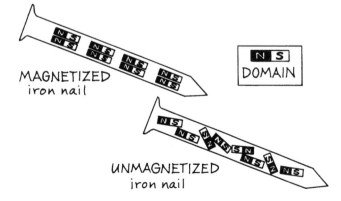

MAGNETIZED
iron nail

UNMAGNETIZED
iron nail

N S
DOMAIN

No one knows when magnetism was first discovered, but there is evidence that the ancient Chinese, Romans, and Greeks all knew about it. It is believed that the Greeks found magnetic stones in an ancient place called Magnesia (in the northeastern part of the Greek peninsula) that could attract pieces of iron. The stones were first called "Magnete stones" after the Magnetes, a Greek people who lived in Magnesia. Later, sailors used the stones to make compasses and called the stones **lodestones,** meaning "leading stones." Today the stones are known to be an iron ore and natural magnet called **magnetite.**

Around 1269 Pierre de Maricourt (c. 1220–1290), a French scientist, discovered that lodestones had two regions of strongest force. He discovered that these regions, which he called poles, **repelled** (pushed away from), and others **attracted** (drew near to), each other. Today it is understood that these are regions, one at each end of a magnet, where the magnetic field is strongest. They are called **magnetic poles;** one magnetic pole is called the **north pole** and the other the **south pole.** Like poles (north and north, or south and south) repel each other, and unlike poles (north and south) attract each other.

In 1600 the English physician and scientist William Gilbert (1544–1603) confirmed these discoveries and concluded, correctly, that Earth itself is a magnet, which explains why one end of the magnetized needle of a **compass** (an instrument for finding direction) always points toward Earth's **magnetic north** pole (the place near Earth's North Pole where the north pole of all magnets is attracted). The other end of the compass needle, the south pole, points toward Earth's **magnetic south pole** (the place near Earth's South Pole where the south pole of all magnets is attracted).

During the 1830s, the English scientist Michael Faraday (1791–1867) introduced the idea of **magnetic lines of force** (a pattern of lines representing the magnetic field around a magnet). These lines extend through the space surrounding a magnet, running from the north pole to the south pole.

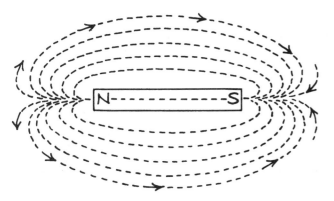

Magnetic Lines of Force

## ACTIVITY: MAGNETIC

### Purpose

To model magnetized and unmagnetized magnetic materials.

### Materials

copy of "Domain Patterns" page 94

scissors

glue stick

two 2-by-6-inch (5-by-15-cm) pieces of corrugated cardboard

marker

3-by-5-inch (7.5-by-12.5-cm) unlined colored index card

## Procedure

1. Make a photocopy of the domain patterns.

2. Cut out 18 of the small domain patterns.

3. Using the glue, stick nine of the domain patterns on one of the cardboard pieces. The domains should be evenly spaced on the cardboard, with like poles of each domain facing in the same direction. Label the cardboard "Magnetized Magnetic Material."

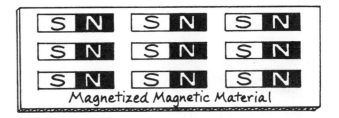

4. Using the glue, randomly stick the remaining nine small domains on the other piece of cardboard. Label the cardboard "Unmagnetized Magnetic Material."

5. Using the marker, make a legend on the index card, called "Domain." Then cut out the large domain pattern and glue it to the card.

# DOMAIN PATTERNS

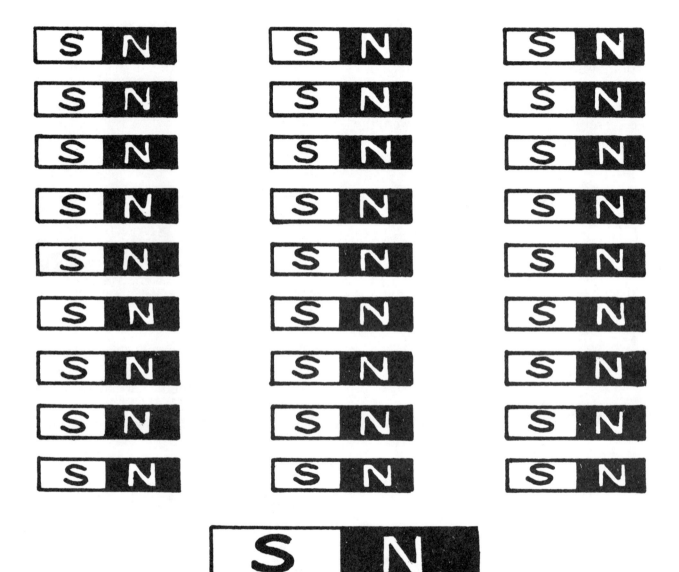

### Results

You have made a model of the domains in a magnetized and an unmagnetized magnetic material.

### Why?

If a magnet is broken into many pieces, each piece, no matter how small, will have a north and a south pole. If the pieces are further broken until they are single atoms, each atom would act like a tiny magnet. Only the atoms in magnetic materials act like magnets. A group of many millions of these tiny atomic magnets lined up parallel to each other with their poles pointing in the same direction form a magnetic domain. Magnetic materials contain domains, while nonmagnetic materials do not. If the domains have a random arrangement, the magnetic material is said to be unmagnetized. But if the domains are lined up parallel to each other with their poles facing in the same direction, the magnetic material is said to be magnetized.

### ON YOUR OWN!

The magnetized and unmagnetized models and legend can be displayed in a box backboard. For instructions on making the backboard, see Appendix 4. Use glue to secure the models and legend to the center panel of the backboard, as shown. Print a title, such as "Line Up," at the top of the backboard.

On the side panel of the backboard, you can display models that show the repulsive force

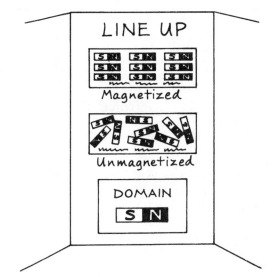

between like poles of a magnet and the attractive force between unlike forces. Use unlined index cards to write information about the attractive and repulsive forces between poles, and glue these cards to the backboard under each model.

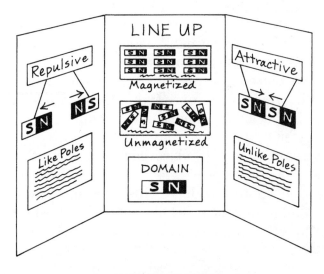

### BOOK LIST

Parker, Steve. *Magnets*. New York: Lorenz Books, 1998. A description of different kinds of magnets and how they are used, as well as experiments using magnets.

VanCleave, Janice. *Janice VanCleave's Magnets*. New York: Wiley, 1993. A collection of fun experiments about magnets.

Vecchione, Glen. *Magnet Science*. New York: Sterling Publications, 1995. An informative book about magnets, including what gives them power to attract or repel each other.

# Easier

## *Make a Model of a Simple Machine!*

Work, as defined by scientists, is done when an object is moved as a result of a force. The amount of work done is the product of the force applied to the object and the distance the object moves. Thus the equation for work is: Work ($W$) = force ($F$) × distance ($d$). If force is measured in newtons and distance is measured in meters, then the work unit is newton-meter or joule (J). For example, if you lift a rock 1 meter using 10 newtons of force, you do 10 joules of work.

A **machine** is a device that helps you do work. Since work is force times distance, a machine helps you by changing the amount or direction of an applied force and/or the direction the object moves. The force applied to a machine is called **effort force** ($F_E$) and the force you and the machine are working against is the **resistance force** ($F_R$), which is often the weight of an object to be moved. Some machines multiply the effort force, which means that a heavy object can be moved with a small effort force.

There are two kinds of distances involved in doing work. One is the distance through which your effort force is applied, called the **effort distance** ($d_E$) The other distance is the **resistance distance** ($d_R$), which is the distance the object is moved. The **mechanical advantage (MA)** of a machine is the number of times a machine increases the effort force. If the mechanical advantage is one, the effort force is equal to the resistance force. If it is more than one, the effort force times the mechanical advantage equals the resistance force. Mechanical

advantage can be determined using either the two kinds of force or the two kinds of distance. Thus the two equations for mechanical advantage are: $MA = (d_E)/(d_R)$ and $MA = (F_R)/(F_E)$. Friction decreases the mechanical advantage of a machine.

There are six types of **simple machines** (the most basic machines): inclined plane, wedge, screw, lever, wheel and axle, and pulley. An **inclined plane** is the simplest of all machines, consisting of a ramp or a similar wedge-shaped device, that makes doing a given amount of work easier. **Inclined** means *tilted* and **plane** means *flat*, so any tilted, flat surface, such as a board raised on one end, is an inclined plane. The length of the plane is the effort distance, and the height the plane is raised is the resistance distance. A ramp, such as those used for wheelchairs, is an inclined plane.

INCLINED PLANE

LOADING

A = Effort Distance
B = Resistance Distance

A **wedge** is an inclined plane that moves. Material is moved up an inclined plane, but a wedge is moved through material. Both have sloping surfaces. For example, a nail is a wedge. When hammered into a board, the pointed or sloping end of the nail moves through the material of the board.

A **screw** is an inclined plane wrapped around a cylinder, forming spiraling ridges. Screws look like spiral staircases. A screw rotates, and with each turn moves a certain distance into a material. The distance the screw moves depends on the screw's **pitch** (the distance between the threads, which are the ridges winding around the screw). The smaller the pitch, the smaller the distance the screw moves, but the greater the mechanical advantage of the screw. Thus a screw with a small pitch is easier to turn.

A **lever** is a rigid bar that is free to rotate about a fixed point called a **fulcrum** (a support about which a lever turns). Levers are divided into three groups: first-class, second-class, and third-class. The classes are based on the locations of the fulcrum, the resistance force, and the effort force, as shown in the diagrams.

moves in a small circle, and the other is a wheel, which moves in a larger circle. The wheel isn't always like a wheel on a car. For example, a screwdriver, a steering wheel, and the crank in the diagram are examples of a wheel and axle machine. When you turn the wheel, your effort force moves in a larger circle than does the axle. Thus the effort distance is greater than the resistance distance. For example, your effort distance in turning the crank would be greater than the resistance distance the bucket moved. The greater the effort distance, the less effort force needed to turn the wheel.

WHEEL AND AXLE

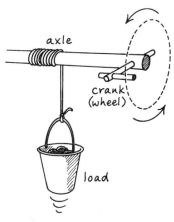

A **pulley** is a lever that rotates about a fixed point. It is made of a wheel, usually grooved, that holds a cord. If you ignore friction, the number of supporting cords on a pulley is equal to its mechanical advantage. Pulleys can be fixed or movable. A **fixed pulley** is secured to one place. A fixed pulley doesn't reduce the amount of effort force needed to move an object, but it makes work easier by changing the direction of a force. The fixed pulley in the diagram has one supporting rope, thus its mechanical advantage is 1. But it is easier to pull down on the cord to raise an object than it would be to lift the object straight up.

LEVERS

A **wheel and axle** is a lever that rotates in a circle. A wheel and axle is made up of parts that move in two circles: one is an axle, which

A **movable pulley** is attached to the object being moved. As the cord is pulled, the pulley

97

and the object move. In the diagram, the movable pulley has two supporting cords, A and B. Thus, the mechanical advantage is two, and you only have to apply half as much effort force to lift the object

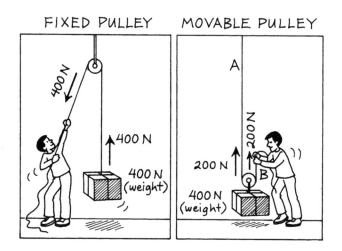

FIXED PULLEY    MOVABLE PULLEY

## ACTIVITY: FIXED

### Purpose

To model a fixed pulley.

### Materials

box backboard (see Appendix 4)
pen
36-inch (90-cm) dowel (the diameter must be small enough to slide through the hole in the thread spool)
large empty thread spool
paper clip
ruler
scissors
string
3-ounce (90-mL) paper cup

### Procedure

1. Prepare a box backboard by following the instructions in Appendix 4.

2. With the pen, make a hole in the middle of each side panel, about 2 inches (5 cm) from the top edge. Hollow the holes with the pen so they are about the same size as the dowel.

3. Push the dowel through one of the holes in the backboard. Place the dowel through the hole in the thread spool, then through the hole in the opposite panel of the backboard. The spool must turn easily on the dowel. Ask an adult to cut off any excess dowel length.

4. Open the paper clip to form a hook, as shown. Cut and tie the end of a 3-foot (10-m) piece of string to the hook.

5. With the pen, make holes on either side of the cup beneath its rim.

6. Cut and tie the ends of a 1-foot (30-cm) piece of string in the holes in the cup, forming a loop.

7. Place the 3-foot piece of string over the thread spool, and place the loop on the cup over the paper clip hook. Then pull down on the free end of the string. Observe the distance the string is pulled down and the distance and direction the cup moves.

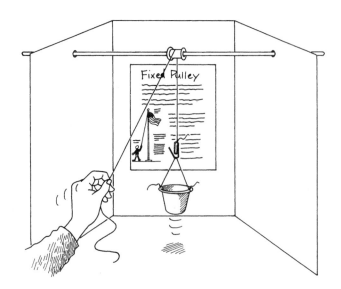

8. Create an information sheet about fixed pulleys and secure it to the center panel behind the fixed pulley model. The information sheet can include an example of a fixed pulley, such as raising a flag on a flagpole, as well as an explanation of how fixed pulleys work.

## Results

You have made a model of a fixed pulley.

## Why?

A **fixed pulley** is a stationary pulley in which the pulley turns as the string moves over the wheel, and a load is raised as the string is pulled. In the model, the spool is the fixed pulley, which turns on the dowel, and the load is the cup. A fixed pulley makes work easier by changing the direction of the effort force. You pull down on the string to raise the load.

## ON YOUR OWN!

Using six index cards, prepare information cards about the six basic simple machines, including definitions, diagrams, and/or pictures representing each. Use glue to attach the cards to the side panels, three on each panel. Title the display "Simple Machines."

## BOOK LIST

Leontovich, M. *Force, of Course.* Glenview, Ill.: GoodYearBooks, 1995. Activities to introduce science at work all around you, including those about machines.

VanCleave, Janice. *Janice VanCleave's Machines.* New York: Wiley, 1993. A collection of fun experiments about machines.

Wiese, Jim. *Rocket Science.* New York: Wiley, 1995. Gadgets that can be made, including machines.

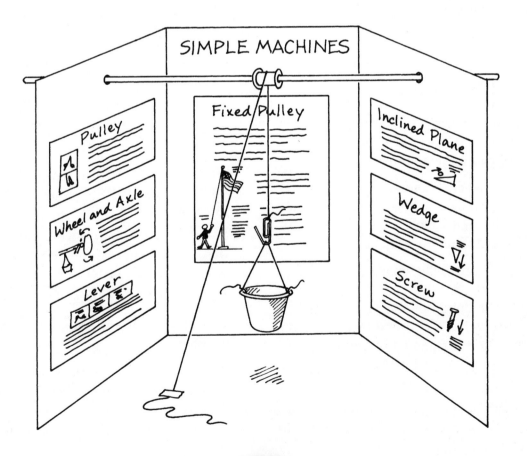

# *Three-Paneled Backboard*

A stand-up backboard provides three panels on which to display material. The title strip makes the topic being displayed readily visible. If a sturdier and/or larger backboard is needed, see Appendix 4, "Box Backboard," or use corrugated cardboard instead of poster board.

## A. NARROW THREE-PANELED BACKBOARD WITH A TITLE STRIP

### Materials

glue
two 22-by-28-inch (55-by-70-cm) pieces of
  poster board
yardstick (meterstick)
pen
scissors

### Procedure

1. Glue the two pieces of poster board together to form one stiff piece of poster board. Allow the glue to dry.

2. Use the yardstick (meterstick) and pen to draw a line across the 28-inch width of the poster board and 4 inches (10 cm) from the top edge. Cut along this line.

3. Draw a line across the small strip cut from the poster board, 4 inches (10 cm) from one end. Cut along this line, and discard the small 4-inch (10 cm) end piece cut from the strip. The remaining 4-by-24-inch (10-by-70-cm) piece of poster board will be your title strip.

4. Use the yardstick (meterstick) and pen to draw two lines from top to bottom down the

large poster board piece, 8 inches (20 cm) from each narrow side. Press firmly with the pen against the poster board to score the paper.

5. Draw two 2-inch (5-cm) lines at the top of the two side panels, and 4 inches (10 cm) from their sides. Cut along these lines to form two notches to hold the title strip.

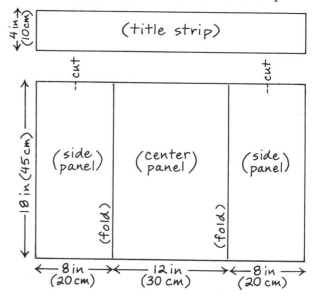

6. Bend the poster board along the two fold lines toward the center of the poster board piece. A three-sided backboard is formed.

7. Stand the backboard on a table and insert the title strip in the notches of the backboard.

8. Papers can be glued inside the backboard.

9. Ideas for making the attached papers more visible:

   • Use contrasting colors, such as white paper and a colored backboard.

   • Mat the papers on colored material. See Appendix 6 for instructions on matting.

## B. WIDE THREE-PANELED BACKBOARD

### Materials

glue
two 20-by-28-inch (50-by-70-cm) pieces of
   poster board
yardstick (meterstick)
pen
scissors

### Procedure

1. Glue the two pieces of poster board together to form one stiff piece of poster board. Allow the glue to dry.

2. Use the yardstick (meterstick) and pen to draw a line across the 28-inch width of the poster board piece, 4 inches (10 cm) from its top edge. Cut along this line. This 4-by-28-inch (10-by-70-cm) piece of poster board will be your title strip.

3. Use the yardstick (meterstick) and pen to draw two lines from top to bottom down the large poster board piece, 6 inches (15 cm) from each narrow side. Press firmly with the pen against the poster board to score the paper.

4. Draw two 2-inch (5-cm) lines at the top of the two side panels and 3 inches (7.5 cm) from their sides. Cut along these lines to form two notches to hold the title strip.

5. Bend the paneled backboard along the two fold lines toward the center of the poster board piece. A three-sided backboard is formed.

6. Stand the backboard on a table and insert the title strip in the notches of the backboard.

7. See steps 8 and 9 in Part A, "Narrow Three-Paneled Backboard," for ideas on attaching papers to the backboard.

# *Layered Book*

Layered books provide a way of displaying a large amount of information in a small space. The overlapping edges create a readily visible table of contents for the book.

## A. FOUR-PAGE LAYERED BOOK

### Materials

ruler
pencil
2 sheets of copy paper
transparent tape

### Procedure

1. Use the ruler and pencil to make a mark on the left side and 1 inch (2.5 cm) from the top of each sheet of paper.

2. Place the two sheets of paper on top of one another, but align the top edge of the top sheet with the mark on the paper below it.

3. Bring the bottom edge of the top sheet up and align its edge with the mark at its top. Press down on the folded edge of the paper.

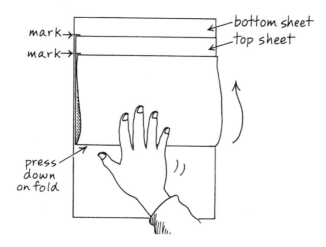

4. Use tape to secure the folded edge to the paper below it.

5. Fold up the bottom paper along the taped fold as shown. Press down on the fold.

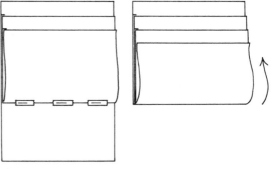

6. The pages of the layered book can be opened to the left or raised, as shown.

## B. SIX-PAGE LAYERED BOOK

Repeat Part A using three sheets of copy paper.

## C. EIGHT- OR TEN-PAGE LAYERED BOOKS

1. Use four sheets of paper for an eight-page book, and five sheets of paper for a 10-page book.

2. Repeat the steps in Part A, making the marks ½ inch (1.25 cm) apart in step 1.

# *Tab Book*

These closed books provide a way of displaying large amounts of information without making your display appear overcrowded. The title on the outside of each book indicates the topic for the information inside the cover. Each book is easily opened and closed so that the display remains neat and orderly.

## A. SMALL TAB BOOK

### Materials

3-by-5-inch (7.5-by-12.5-cm) unlined index card
ruler
pen

### Procedure

1. On the index card, use the ruler and pen to draw a line from top to bottom, ½ inch (1.25 cm) from the end of one of the narrow sides. The ½-inch (1.25-cm) strip across the end of the card will be the tab.

2. Fold the card so that the end of the short side lines up with the tab on the line. Crease the fold.

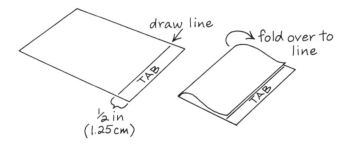

3. Fold the ½-inch (1.25-cm) tab over as shown. Crease the fold.

4. Close the tab book by folding the tab over the shorter side of the card.

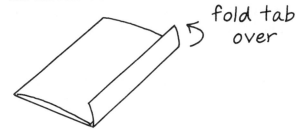

5. Information can be written inside each tab book, and the tab books can be glued to a display.

## B. LARGE TAB BOOK

### Materials

sheet of copy paper
ruler
pen

### Procedure

1. On the paper, use the ruler and pen to draw a line across and 1 inch (2.5 cm) from the end of one of the narrow sides. The 1-inch (2.5-cm) strip across the bottom of the paper will be the tab.

2. Fold the sheet in half, placing the short side opposite the tab on the line. Crease the fold.

3. Fold the 1-inch (1.25-cm) tab over as before. Crease the fold.

4. Close the tab book by folding the tab over the shorter side of the paper.

5. Information can be written inside each tab book, and the tab books can be glued to a display.

# *Box Backboard*

Some displays require a single stand-up backboard. A box can easily be used for this, and the size of the box you select depends on the size of the material being displayed.

## Materials

open box, such as one that holds copy paper
yardstick (meterstick)
scissors
tape
glue
bulletin board paper or butcher paper
(in a color of your choice)

## Procedure

**1.** Open the box by pulling the overlapping pieces apart.

**2.** Cut off the cardboard pieces attached to the bottom and the two largest sides of the box. A three-paneled backboard will be left.

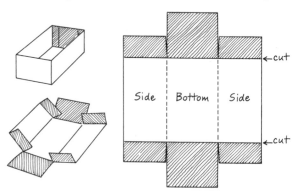

**3.** Use the yardstick (meterstick) and scissors to cut a piece of bulletin board paper. The length of the paper should be twice the width of the three-paneled backboard plus 2 inches (5 cm). The width of the paper should be the height of the backboard plus 4 inches. For example, the three-paneled backboard

made from a copy paper box has a width of 29.5 inches (73.75 cm) and a height of 17 inches (42.5 cm). So the paper size should be:
Length = $(29.5 \times 2) + 2 = 61$ inches (152.5 cm)
Width = $17 + 4 = 21$ inches (52.5 cm)

**4.** Lay the paper backboard on a flat surface, such as a table or a floor.

**5.** Cover the entire front edges and the folds of the backboard with glue.

**6.** Lay the backboard in the center of the paper, glue side down as shown.

**7.** Turn the backboard over.

**8.** Fold over the extra paper at the ends of the backboard, covering the back of the backboard. Secure the paper with tape.

**9.** Fold the extra paper at the top and bottom of the backboard over the edge, toward the back of the backboard, and secure with tape. Press the paper so that it forms a smooth layer over the front of the backboard.

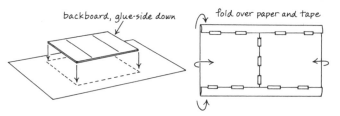

**10.** Stand the backboard and bend the side panels in to support it.

# Flap Book

Flap books provide a way to display facts in a sequence. They also allow only one part of the information to be viewed at a time.

## Materials

ruler

pen

8-by-8-inch (20-by-20-cm) square piece of poster board

scissors

10-by-10-inch (25-by-25-cm) square piece of colored poster board (your choice of color)

*Note: Any size squares can be used, but the larger square should be 2 inches greater than the smaller one.*

## Procedure

1. Use the ruler and pen to draw two diagonal lines across the small square of paper from opposite corners. Press down with the pen when drawing the lines to score the paper so that the paper will be easy to fold along the lines in a later step.

2. Make a dot on each line 1 inch (2.5 cm) from the corner of the paper.

3. Use the ruler and pen to connect the dots, parallel to the outside edges. Again, press down with the pen to score the paper.

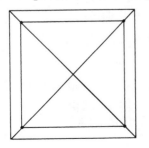

4. Fold the small square along one of the diagonal lines.

5. Cut from the fold along the diagonal to the dot as shown.

6. Unfold the paper and refold along the other diagonal line. Then repeat step 5.

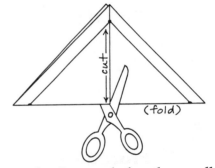

7. Close the flaps and glue the small square to the larger square by placing glue around the edges of the small square, centering the smaller square within the larger square. Allow the glue to dry.

8. Fold the four triangular flaps outward and crease the fold of each.

9. The area beneath each flap can be used for written information and/or pictures.

10. Close the flaps. The flaps can be numbered to indicate the order in which they are to be raised.

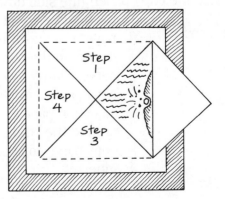

# *Matting*

A border around information sheets, pictures, and/or diagrams makes them more attractive than when they are displayed alone. Matting makes information displayed appear neater as well as more eye-catching.

## A. FULL SHEET

### Materials

1 sheet of white copy paper
1 sheet of 9-by-12-inch (22.5-by-30-cm) colored construction paper
pencil
glue stick

### Procedure

**1.** Lay the copy paper on the colored construction paper.

**2.** Move the copy paper so that it is in the center of the colored paper.

**3.** Use the pencil to draw a line on the colored paper by tracing along one of the short sides of the copy paper.

**4.** Remove the copy paper and spread about a 1-inch (2.5-cm) strip of glue along the four sides of the copy paper.

**5.** Place the copy paper glue side down so that the short edge of the copy paper touches the line drawn on the construction paper. Slowly lower the copy paper onto the construction paper. Rub around the edges of the copy paper to secure the glue.

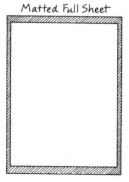

Matted Full Sheet

## B. LONG HALF-SHEET

### Materials

1 sheet of white copy paper
scissors
5-by-12-inch (12.5-by-30-cm) piece of colored construction paper
glue stick

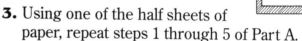

Matted
Long Half Sheet

### Procedure

**1.** Fold the copy paper in half lengthwise.

**2.** Unfold the paper and cut along the fold.

**3.** Using one of the half sheets of paper, repeat steps 1 through 5 of Part A.

## C. SHORT HALF-SHEET

### Materials

1 sheet of white copy paper
scissors
7-by-10-inch (17.5-by-25-cm) piece of colored construction paper
glue stick

### Procedure

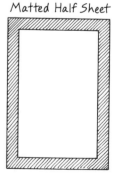

Matted Half Sheet

**1.** Fold the copy paper in half from top to bottom.

**2.** Unfold the paper and cut along the fold.

**3.** Using one of the half sheets of paper, repeat steps 1 through 5 of Part A.

# *Tent Stand*

Some information needs to be on a stand, such as legends and/or information cards for 3-D models. A tent stand allows you to change the information card if needed during an oral presentation.

## Materials

pencil
ruler
6-by-13-inch (15-by-32.5 cm) piece of poster board
transparent tape

## Procedure

**1.** Use the pencil and ruler to draw four lines across the piece of poster board. Measuring from one of the short sides, make the lines 1 inch (2.5 cm), 4 inches (10 cm), 8 inches (20 cm), and 12 inches (30 cm) from the end.

**2.** Fold the paper down along lines A, B, and C.

**3.** Fold the paper up along line D.

**4.** Use tape to secure tab A to the back of face B, as shown.

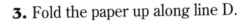

**5.** Set the stand on its bottom and bend up tab B to form a holder. Information cards or small models can be placed on the stand.

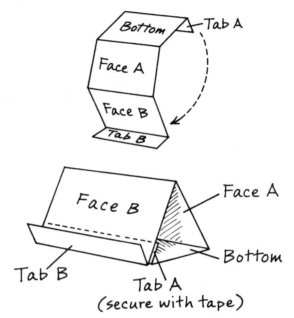

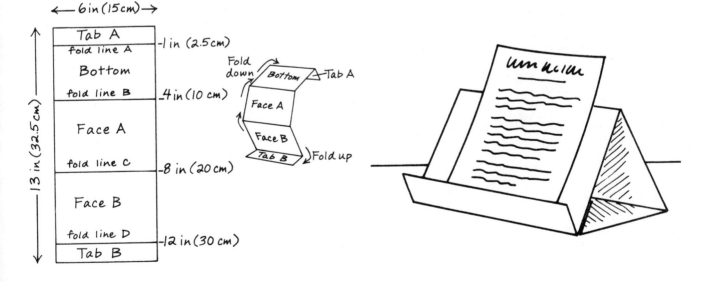

# *Lifter*

An accordion-shaped strip of paper is used to lift flat figures, forming a 3-D diagram. One end of the lifter is attached to the background of the diagram, and the picture or drawing to be raised is attached to the other end of the lifter.

## Materials

scissors
index card
glue
¾-inch (1.87-cm) round label

## Procedure

**1.** Cut a strip from the index card about one-third as wide and about one-third longer than the object being lifted. For example, a ¾ -(1.87-cm) round label needs a lifter about ¼ inch (0.63 cm) wide and about 1 inch (2.5 cm) long. Note that the size of the strip does not have to be exact.

**2.** Fold the paper strip accordion style, forming an N shape. This is the lifter.

**3.** Place a dot of glue on one end of the lifter and press this glue-covered end against the background of the diagram where you want to put the figure to be raised.

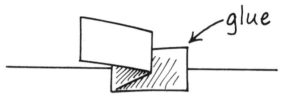

**4.** Allow the glue to dry, then stick the label on the other end of the paper lifter. If the object being raised doesn't have a sticky side like the label, then use glue to secure it to the end of the lifter.

# *Pyramid*

A pyramid display can be used right side up or turned on its side. When right side up, the pyramid can stand on its open base or be hung from its vertex, providing three sides to display information. When hanging, it can be used much like a mobile with objects hanging from each side. On its side, the pyramid provides a two-sided backboard on which information can be displayed and a floor on which to set models.

## A. PAPER PYRAMID

### Materials

sheet of copy paper
scissors
transparent tape

### Procedure

1. Fold the paper as shown with its top edge against an adjacent side. Crease the fold by pressing it flat with your fingers.

2. Cut off and discard the bottom strip from the paper.

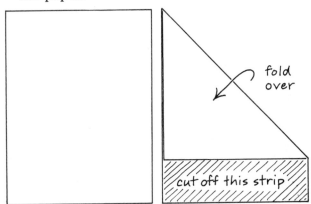

fold over

cut off this strip

3. Unfold the paper and refold it diagonally the opposite way. Crease the fold as before, then unfold the paper.

4. Cut along one of the folds to the center of the paper, forming triangles A and B, as shown in the diagram.

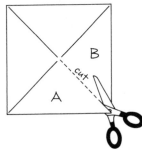

5. Overlap triangle B with triangle A and secure them together with tape.

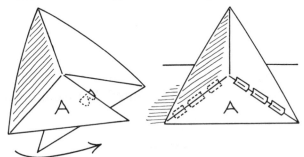

6. Stand the paper structure on its open base, and you have a pyramid.

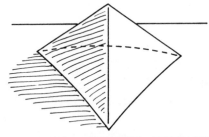

## B. POSTER BOARD PYRAMID

### Materials

yardstick (meterstick)
pen
square piece of poster board
scissors

## Procedure

1. Use the yardstick (meterstick) and pen to draw tow diagonal lines across the poster board square. Press firmly with the pen against the poster board to score the paper.

2. Fold the poster board square along one of the diagonal lines. Crease the fold by pressing it flat with your fingers.

3. Unfold the paper and fold along the other diagonal line. Crease the fold as before.

4. Follow steps 4 through 6 in Part A, "Paper Pyramid."

## C. POSTER BOARD PYRAMID BACKBOARD

### Materials

yardstick (meterstick)
pen
square piece of poster board
scissors

### Procedure

1. Make a poster board pyramid using the procedure in part B.

2. To use the pyramid as a backboard, stand the pyramid on one of its faces.

3. If you wish to attach paper to the pyramid backboard, cut a sheet of copy paper into two parts diagonally. Information can be written on these pieces, and the pieces can be glued inside the backboard as shown.

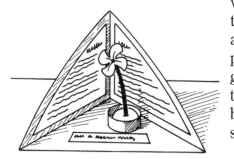

4. Ideas for making the attached papers more visible:

   • Use contrasting colors, such as white paper and a colored backboard.

   • Mat the papers on colored material. See Appendix 6 for instructions on matting.

## D. HANGING PYRAMID

### Materials

scissors
ruler
string
paper or poster board pyramid from Part A or Part B
transparent tape

### Procedure

1. Measure and cut a piece of string at least 4 inches (10 cm) longer than needed to hang the display.

2. Open the pyramid and attach the string to face B as shown.

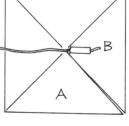

3. Overlap triangle B with triangle A and secure them together with tape. Tape or tie the string to a support to hang the pyramid.

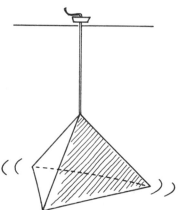

# *Scale Model*

Use this procedure to create a scale for a model that is smaller than the actual object.

## Materials

calculator
paper
pencil
compass

## Procedure

1. Look at the largest and smallest measurements, then determine the scale that will be used for the model. For example, Earth's three layers have these measurements:

core: diameter = 6,800 km (4,259 miles)
mantle: width = 2,900 km (1,812 miles)
crust: width = 5 to 70 km (3 to 44 miles)

The crust measurement is so small that it cannot be considered in determining the scale. The crust therefore can be a thin, unmeasured layer on the model. So, considering only the measurements of the core's diameter and mantle's width, experiment with scales. It is easier to use metric measurements for scale models because portions of a whole number are easily measured. Since the core and mantle measurements are both more than 1,000 km, a scale of 1 cm = 1,000 km could be used. Use the scale to calculate the size of each part. Do this by multiplying the actual size of each part by the scale multiple:

- Core size:

6,800 × 1 cm/1,000 km = 6.8 cm

- Mantle size:

2,900 km × 1cm/1,000 km = 2.9 cm

2. Draw a diagram showing each part and its scale size. In the drawing shown, the diameter of the outside layer is determined to be 12.6 cm, which is about 5 inches. A completed model with a thin outer layer to represent the crust would still be less than 6 inches (15 cm) in diameter.

EARTH'S LAYERS

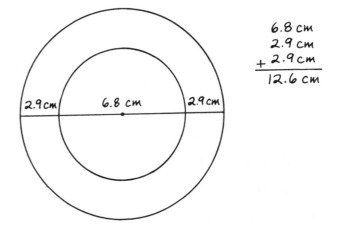

3. To make a model twice as large, use a scale multiple that is half as large. For example, to make the model about 12 inches in diameter, use this scale multiple: 1 cm/500 km.

- Core size:

6,800 × 1 cm/500 km = 13.6 cm

- Mantle size:

2,900 km × 1 cm/500 km = 5.8 cm

The diameter of the model would be 13.6 cm + 5.8 cm + 5.8 cm = 25.2 cm. This is about 12 inches (30 cm).

# *Large Circle*

Protractors work well when drawing small circles, but use this procedure for drawing large circles.

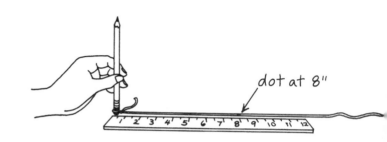

dot at 8″

## Materials

    ruler

    scissors

    string

    2 pencils

    marker

    transparent tape

    paper (width and depth at least 1 inch (2.5 cm) greater than the diameter of the circle to be drawn)

## Procedure

1. Measure and cut a piece of string at least 4 inches (10 cm) longer than the radius of the circle to be drawn.

2. Tie a loop in one end of the string.

3. Lay the ruler on a table. Place the string next to it with the loop at the zero end of the ruler.

4. Stand one of the pencils in the center of the loop, eraser end down.

5. Use the marker to make a dot on the string at the length equal to the radius of the circle to be drawn. For example, in the diagram the dot is made at 8 inches (20 cm). Try to keep the string taut.

6. Starting at the dot on the string, use tape to secure the free end of the string to the second pencil.

7. Place the string on the paper with the loop in the center of the paper.

8. Stand the first pencil, eraser end down, in the loop.

9. Pull the pencil taped to the string outward to stretch the string.

10. Move the taped pencil around with its point pressed against the paper until a complete circle is drawn. The radius of the circle will equal the length of the string.

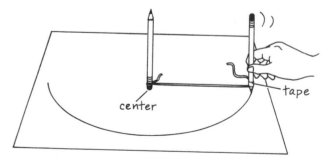

center      tape

# *Circle Stand*

Use this procedure to construct a stand for information cards made from index cards or other stiff material. The stand can be placed next to 3-D models.

## Materials

ruler
pencil
3-by-10-inch (7.5-by-25-cm) strip of poster board
scissors
transparent tape

## Procedure

**1.** Use the ruler and pencil to draw a 1-by-4-inch (2.5-by-5-cm) rectangle in the center of one of the long sides of the poster board strip.

**2.** Cut out the rectangle and discard it. Cut a slit about ½ inch (1.25 cm) long in the bottom two corners where the rectangle was cut out, as shown.

**3.** Tape the ends of the poster board strip together, forming a circle. You have made a circle stand.

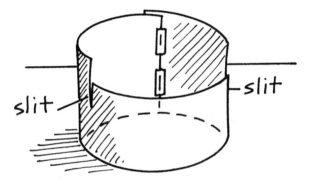

**4.** Use the circle stand by inserting an information card in the slit openings.

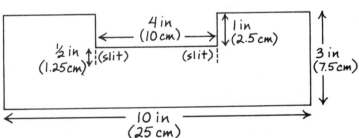

# Glossary

**accelerate** To increase speed.

**acid** A chemical that breaks up when added to water, first forming a hydrogen ion. The hydrogen ions combine with water, forming hydronium ions; acids taste sour.

**active** In reference to volcanos, a volcano that has erupted within the last century.

**air** The name of the mixture of gases in Earth's atmosphere, including nitrogen and oxygen, that supports life as we know it.

**alkali** Another name for **base.**

**amorphous solid** A solid that doesn't have an ordered internal structure; solids without crystal lattices.

**angiosperm** A flowering plant.

**anion** A negatively charged ion.

**anther** The part of the stamen that produces pollen grains.

**aperture** For telescopes, it is the diameter of the light-collecting lens in a refracting telescope or the primary mirror in a reflecting telescope.

**asterism** A group of stars with a shape within a constellation.

**asteroids** Minor planets; small rocky bodies that orbit the Sun, mainly between the orbits of Mars and Jupiter.

**athenosphere** A semisolid layer of Earth that makes up the upper part of the mantle, between the mesosphere and the lithosphere.

**atmosphere** The blanket of gas surrounding a celestial body.

**atom** The smallest building block of an element that retains the properties of the element.

**attract** Draw together.

**autumn** The climatic season between summer and winter with cool days and nights.

**autumn equinox** The first day of autumn, on or about September 23, in the Northern Hemisphere.

**average kinetic energy** Thermal energy divided by the total number of particles.

**axis** The imaginary line through the center of a body about which the body rotates.

**bacteria** Unicellular organisms made of prokaryotic cells.

**balance** An instrument used to measure mass.

**ball-and-socket** A movable joint that allows movement in different ways, such as the joint between your thigh and hip bones.

**base** A chemical that breaks up when added to water, forming hydroxide ions; bases taste bitter.

**battery** A device that uses chemicals to produce electricity.

**biceps** The large flexor muscle on the front side of your upper arm; the muscle that raises the forearm.

**blood** A tissue in vertebrates made up of several types of blood cells suspended in a liquid called plasma. Blood transports oxygen and nutrients to cells and throughout the body and carries wastes away from cells.

**blood vessels** Tubelike organs in an organism through which blood flows.

**boiling point** The temperature at which vaporization occurs throughout a liquid.

**bronchi** Respiratory organs consisting of short tubes that direct air into the lungs.

**cardiac muscles** Involuntary muscles found only in the heart and made up of tightly woven cells.

**carpel** The female reproductive organ in a plant.

**cartilage** A firm but flexible tissue that gives shape and support to the bodies of some animals.

**cation** A positively charged ion.

**celestial bodies** The natural things in the sky, such as stars, suns, moons, and planets.

**cell membrane** The thin outer skin of the cell that holds the cell together, protects the inner parts, and allows materials to move into and out of the cell.

**cells** The building blocks of organisms; the smallest structure that is able to perform life processes, such as taking in nutrients, giving off waste, and reproducing.

**cemented** Stuck together.

**charge** The property of particles within atoms that cause a force between the particles; also called **electric charge.**

**chemicals** A substance or mixture of substances.

**chrysalis** The protective covering for the pupa of certain insects, especially butterflies.

**cinder cone volcano** A volcano formed by an explosive eruption in which tephra piles up into a steep-sided, loosely packed cone.

**circulatory system** Body parts, including the heart and blood vessels, that work together to transport blood throughout the body.

**climatic seasons** Divisions of the year based on temperature changes.

**closed circuit** An electric circuit in which the path formed by conductors is continuous.

**cocoon** The protective silk covering for the pupa stage of many insects, especially moths.

**comet** A body of dust, gases, and ice that moves in an extremely elongated orbit around the sun.

**compacted** Packed together.

**compass** An instrument for finding direction, with a magnetic needle that always points north.

**complete flower** A flower that has these four basic parts: stamens, carpel (pistil), petals, and sepals.

**complete metamorphosis** See **metamorphosis, complete.**

**composite volcano** A cone-shaped volcano formed by alternating layers of solidified lava and rock particles; a volcano that is a combination of a cinder cone and shield volcano.

**compound** A substance made of two or more different elements; See **ionic compound** and **molecular compound.**

**compound joints** Several joints between bones that work together to allow the bones to move in different directions.

**compress** To press together.

**compression** Squeezing forces that push rocks together, causing them to rumple, fold, and sometimes break.

**concave** Curved inward, like the surface of a plate.

**concentration** The amount of matter per unit volume.

**condense** The change of a gas to a liquid.

**conductor** A material that easily allows heat or electric charges to pass through it.

**connective tissue** Tissue that holds internal body parts, including bones, together.

**constellation** A group of stars that appears to make patterns in the sky.

**contract** To shorten.

**convex** Curved outward, like the surface of a ball.

**core** The center layer of Earth believed to be made mostly of two metals, iron and nickel. This inner layer is about 2,125 miles (3,400 km) thick.

**crater** (1) The depression at the top of a volcano. (2) A bowl-shaped depression in the surface of a celestial body. See **impact crater.**

**crescent phase** The Moon phase in which there is a small lighted area resembling a segment of a ring with pointed ends.

**crust** The outermost layer of Earth that is about 44 miles (70 km) thick in some mountainous regions and averages about 5 miles (8 km) under the ocean.

**crystal lattice** The rigid, orderly arrangement of particles in a crystalline solid.

**crystalline solid** A solid made of crystal lattices.

**cubic centimeter (cm³)** A common metric volume unit determined by multiplying length × width × height measured in centimeters.

**cubit** The distance between the elbow and the tip of the middle finger.

**current electricity** The movement of electric charges.

**cushioning** In reference to bones, it is soft padding material that prevents excessive pressure or rubbing together of the bones.

**cyanobacteria** Unicellular organisms made of prokaryotic cells; formerly called blue-green algae.

**cytoplasm** A clear, jellylike material made mostly of water, occupying the region between the nucleus and the cell membrane, containing substances and particles that work together to sustain life.

**debris** The scattered pieces of something that has been broken.

**density** The measure of the mass or weight of a given volume of a material.

**diatomic molecule** A molecule made of two atoms of like or unlike elements.

**dilute** To add water to a solution made with water.

**diorama** A 3-D miniature scene with figures placed in front of a painted background.

**dip-slip fault** A fault in which movement is vertical and the fault plane is usually at a slant. See **normal fault** and **reverse fault.**

**domains** Groups of atoms in magnets or magnetic material that act like tiny magnets.

**dormant** In reference to a volcano, it is a volcano that has been inactive for several hundred years, but could become active.

**Earth day** Twenty-four hours.

**Earth year** Three hundred sixty-five days.

**earthquake** Shaking of the ground caused by rapid movement of Earth's crust.

**effort distance ($d_E$)** The distance through which an effort force is applied.

**effort force ($f_E$)** The force applied to a machine.

**egg** (1) The first stage of metamorphosis. (2) A female reproductive cell.

**ejecta blanket** The ejected material of a meteorite that falls back to the surface, partially filling an impact crater and forming a layer around it.

**elbow** The joint that connects the bones of your upper and lower arm.

**electric charge** The property of particles within atoms that causes the particles to attract or repel one another. There are two types of electric charges, a positive charge and a negative charge. See **proton** and **electron.**

**electric circuit** The path through which electric charges move.

**electricity** A form of energy associated with the presence and movement of electrical charges.

**electron** A negatively charged particle spinning around the outside of an atom's nucleus.

**element** A substance made of only one kind of atom. See **natural elements** and **synthetic elements.**

**endoplasmic reticulum (ER)** A network of tubes that manufacture, process, and transport materials within cells containing a nucleus. The ER connects to the nuclear membrane and extends into the cytoplasm. There are two types of ER: rough and smooth. Rough ER is covered with **ribosomes.**

**energy** The ability of an object to cause changes, or the ability to do work.

**energy conversion** The change of energy from one form to another.

**equator** Imaginary line midway between the North and South Poles that divides Earth into two parts: the Northern Hemisphere and the Southern Hemisphere.

**eukaryotic cell**   A cell with a nucleus found in most organisms and all multicellular organisms, including plants and animals.

**evaporate**   The change of a liquid to a gas at a liquid's surface.

**exoskeleton**   The outer covering of an insect.

**extensor**   A muscle that straightens a joint.

**extinct**   In reference to a volcano, it is a volcano that has not erupted in thousands of years and most likely will never again become active.

**eyepiece**   The lens of a telescope that one looks through.

**fault**   A large fracture in rock layers of Earth formed when rocks not only break but also move along either side of the break.

**fault block**   The rock on either side of a fault plane.

**fault plane**   The fracture line of a fault.

**fertilization**   The union of a sperm and an egg.

**filament**   (1) The stalklike portion of a stamen that supports the anther. (2) A small wire inside an electric lamp that glows when hot, producing light.

**first quarter phase**   The Moon phase in which half of the side of the Moon facing Earth is lighted; the moon phase after one-fourth of a lunar month has passed.

**fixed joints**   Joints that allow no movement, such as those in the skull.

**fixed pulley**   A stationary pulley in which the pulley turns as the string moves over the wheel, and a load is raised as the string is pulled.

**flexor**   A muscle that bends a joint.

**flower**   The reproductive system of an angiosperm.

**focal point**   The point where light rays passing through a lens meet.

**foot**   (1) A length measurement originally equal to the length of a person's foot, which was first divided into 16 parts and later into 12 parts. (2) A modern measurement equal to 12 inches.

**footwall**   In reference to a fault with vertical motion, it is the fault block below the fault plane.

**forearm**   The lower part of your arm, between the elbow and the wrist.

**formula**   The combination of symbols of elements used to represent a molecule.

**fracture**   To break with rough or jagged edges.

**freeze**   The change of a liquid to a solid.

**freezing point**   The freezing temperature of a liquid.

**friction**   The force that opposes the motion of two surfaces in contact with each other.

**fulcrum**   The support about which a lever turns.

**full moon**   A phase of the Moon when the side of the Moon facing Earth is lighted.

**galaxy**   A group of millions of stars, gas, dust, and other celestial bodies.

**gas**   The state of matter with no definite shape or volume.

**golgi bodies**   Cell structures where protein is stored until needed.

**geocentric**   Earth-centered.

**gibbous phase**   The Moon phase in which more than half of the side of the Moon facing Earth is lighted.

**gliding joints**   Joints in which the bones move easily over one another, such as in the wrist and between vertebrae.

**goose bump**   A small bump on the skin around a hair, created by the contraction of smooth muscles attached to the hair.

**gram (g)**   The basic metric mass unit.

**gravitational acceleration**   Acceleration due to gravity; Earth's gravitational acceleration is about 32 ft/sec$^2$ (9.8 m/sec$^2$).

**gravitational potential energy (GPE)**   Potential energy due to the height of an object above a surface.

**gravity**   The force that pulls objects together.

**gravity rate (GR)**   In reference to a celestial body, it is the gravity of the body divided by Earth's gravity.

**hanging wall**   In reference to a fault with vertical motion, it is the fault block above a fault plane.

**heat**   Energy that is transferred from a warm material to a cool material.

**heliocentric**   Sun-centered.

**hinge joint**   A joint than can move in one direction, like the hinge on a door, such as the joints in your knees, elbows, and fingers.

**horizon**   A line where the sky seems to meet Earth.

**hydronium ion, $H_3O^+$**   An ion formed when an acid is dissolved in water.

**hydroxide, $OH^{-1}$**   An ion formed when a base is dissolved in water.

**igneous rock**   Rock produced by the cooling and solidifying of liquid rock.

**image**   The likeness of an object formed by a lens or a mirror.

**impact crater**   A bowl-shaped depression caused by the impact of a solid body.

**imperial system**   A standard system of measurement established in 1305 by King Edward I of England.

**inch**   A length measurement. The word originated from the Roman measurement of *uncia*. The modern measurement is equal to $\frac{1}{12}$ of a foot.

**inclined**   Tilted.

**inclined plane**   A ramp or a similar wedge-shaped device that makes doing a given amount of work easier; a simple machine.

**incomplete flower**   A flower that lacks one or more of these four basic flower parts: stamens, carpel (pistil), petals, and sepals.

**incomplete metamorphosis**   See **metamorphosis, incomplete.**

**indicator**   A chemical that changes color in an acid and/or a base.

**inferior planets**   Planets whose orbit lies closer than Earth's orbit to the Sun; Mercury and Venus.

**inner core**   The solid inner layer of Earth's core and an area with the greatest pressure and temperature.

**inorganic**   A substance that isn't alive, was never alive, and was not made by life processes.

**involuntary muscles**   Muscles that cannot be controlled at will.

**ion**   An atom or group of atoms that has a positive or negative charge.

**ionic compound**   A compound made of anions and cations.

**joint**   (1) A place where two bones meet. See **fixed joints, movable joints,** and **slightly movable joints.** (2) A large fracture in rock layers of Earth with no movement of the rock along either side of the break.

**kinetic energy (KE)**   The energy that an object has because of its motion.

**larva** (plural **larvae**)   A wormlike active second stage of metamorphosis.

**lateral fault**   A fault produced by shearing, in which the movement of the fault blocks along a vertical fault plane is mainly horizontal, to the left or right, with little to no up-and-down movement. Also called a **strike-slip fault.**

**latitude**   The distance in degrees north and south of the equator, which is at 0° latitude.

**lava**   Molten rock from inside Earth that reaches Earth's surface.

**left lateral fault**   Relative to an observer standing on one of the fault blocks, it is a lateral fault in which the other block moves to the left.

**length**   The distance from one point to another.

**lever**   A rigid bar that is free to rotate about a fixed point called a **fulcrum;** a simple machine.

**ligament**   A tough band of slightly elastic connective tissue that holds bones.

**liquid**   The state of matter with a definite volume but no definite shape.

**liter (L)**   A basic metric volume unit equal to 1,000 cm³.

**lithosphere**   The solid outer layer of Earth above the athenosphere.

**lodestone**   Magnetite. A magnetic stone used to make a compass; also known as a leading stone.

**lubricant**   A substance that reduces friction between materials in contact with each other, such as bones at movable joints.

**lunar month**   The time between two new moons; about 29 days.

**lungs**   Respiratory organs where gas is exchanged.

**lysosomes**   Sacs found in cells that contain chemicals used to destroy harmful substances or worn-out cell parts. Numerous in disease-fighting cells, such as white blood cells, that destroy harmful invaders or cell debris.

**machine**   A device that helps you do work.

**magma chamber**   The pool of molten rock deep within Earth.

**magnet**   An object that attracts iron and other magnetic materials, including cobalt and nickel.

**magnetic field**   The space around a magnet which affects magnetic material and/or another magnet.

**magnetic force**   The attraction that magnets have for each other or magnetic materials; also called **magnetism.**

**magnetic lines of force**   A pattern of lines representing the magnetic field around a magnet.

**magnetic north pole**   The place near Earth's North Pole that attracts the north pole of all magnets.

**magnetic pole**   The regions on a magnet where the magnetic field is strongest. See **north pole** and **south pole.**

**magnetic south pole**   The place near Earth's South Pole that attracts the south pole of all magnets.

**magnetism**   See **magnetic force.**

**magnetite**   A magnetic stone made of iron ore. Also called a **lodestone.**

**major planets**   Planets with diameters larger than Ceres, the largest asteroid; Mercury, Venus, Earth, Mars, Jupiter, Saturn, Uranus, Neptune, and Pluto.

**mantle**   The middle and the largest layer of Earth, with a thickness of about 1,812 miles (2,900 km). The most common chemicals found in this layer are silicates.

**mass**   An amount of matter making up a material.

**matter**   Anything that occupies space and has mass.

**mechanical advantage (MA)**   The number of times a machine increases the effort force.

**mechanical energy**   The energy of motion; the energy of an object that is moving or is capable of motion; the sum of the kinetic and potential energy of an object.

**melt**   To change from a solid to a liquid.

**melting point**   The temperature at which a substance changes from a solid to a liquid.

**mesosphere**   A solid layer of Earth starting at the boundary of the outer core and making up most of the mantle.

**metamorphic rock**   Rock that has been changed by great heat and pressure within Earth's crust.

**metamorphosis, complete**   The four-stage process of insect development from egg to larva to pupa to adult.

**metamorphosis, incomplete**   The three-stage process of insect development, from egg to nymph to adult.

**meteor**   A meteoroid that has entered the atmosphere of a celestial body; the streak of light produced by a vaporizing meteoroid as it passes through Earth's atmosphere; commonly called a shooting star.

**meteorite**   A meteor that hits the surface of Earth or any celestial body.

**meteoroids**   All the solid debris in our solar system orbiting the Sun.

**meter (m)**   A basic metric length unit.

**mineral**   A substance made of a single kind of element or chemical compound with these basic characteristics: (1) it occurs naturally; (2) it is inorganic; (3) it has a definite chemical composition; and (4) it is a crystalline solid.

**minor planets**   Asteroids; small rocky bodies that orbit the Sun.

**mitochondria**   The power station of a cell where food and oxygen react to produce the energy needed for the cells to work and live.

**model**   A representation of an existing object or system, including diagrams and three-dimensional structures.

**molecular compound**   A compound made of like molecules.

**molecule**   A particle made of two or more atoms linked together; the smallest particle of a molecular compound.

**molting**   A process of shedding an exoskeleton.

**moon**   A body that revolves around a planet and shines only by the light it reflects. The name of Earth's moon is the Moon.

**moon phases**   The repeating shapes of the sunlit surface of the Moon facing Earth.

**movable joints**   Joints that are able to move freely.

**movable pulley**   A pulley that is attached to the object being moved.

**multicellular**   Made of many cells.

**muscle**   The tissue responsible for motion.

**natural elements**   Elements that occur in nature, such as carbon, oxygen, nitrogen, and mercury.

**nectar**   A sugary liquid produced in many flowers at the base of their petals, which is food for many insects.

**negative terminal**   A terminal with a negative charge.

**neutral**   Having no acidic or basic properties.

**new moon**   The phase of the Moon when the side of the Moon facing Earth is not illuminated.

**newton**   Metric unit of weight.

**Newtonian telescope**   See **reflecting telescope.**

**noncrystalline solid**   A solid that is not made of crystal lattices and is amorphous.

**normal fault**   A dip-slip fault caused by tension in which the hanging wall moves down in relationship to the footwall.

**northern circumpolar constellations**   Constellations in the Northern Hemisphere that contain northern circumpolar stars; constellations that are always above the horizon, and seem to rotate around Polaris.

**northern circumpolar stars**   Stars in the Northern Hemisphere that are always above the horizon and rotate around Polaris.

**Northern Hemisphere**   The area north of the equator.

**North Pole**   The north end of Earth's axis.

**north pole**   The end of a magnet attracted to the magnetic north pole of Earth.

**North Star**   Polaris; the star that the north end of Earth's axis points toward.

**nose**   A respiratory organ where air enters the body.

**nucleus**   (1) The spherical or oval-shaped body in a cell that houses the things that control cell activity. (2) The central area of an atom, containing positively charged protons.

**nymph**   A young insect that looks like the adult, but is smaller and wingless.

**objective lens**   A lens at the end of a telescope pointed toward an object being viewed.

**open circuit**   An electric circuit in which there is a break in the path formed by conductors.

**orbit**   (1) The curved path of one celestial body around another, such as planets around the Sun. (2) To move in a curved path around another body; revolve.

**organ**   A group of different tissues working together to perform a special job.

**organelles**   The small organs in the cytoplasm of a cell that work together to sustain life.

**organism**   A living thing.

**organ system**   A group of organs working together to perform a special job.

**outer core**   The liquid outer layer of Earth's core.

**ovary**   The rounded base of a pistil where seeds are formed.

**ovules**   Seedlike parts in the ovary of a plant pistil that contain eggs.

**parallel circuit**   An electric circuit in which the electric current has more than one path to follow.

**pedicel**   The stem that connects a flower to the rest of the plant.

**pendulum**   A weight hung so that it is free to swing about a fixed point.

**petals**   The leaflike structures that surround and help protect a flower's reproductive organs.

**pH scale**   A special scale for measuring the acidic or basic nature of a substance.

**physical change**   A change in which the physical properties of a substance may be changed, but the particles making up the substances are not changed.

**physical properties**   Characteristics of a substance that can be measured and/or observed without changing the makeup of the substance.

**pistil**   See **carpel.**

**pitch**   The distance between the threads on a screw.

**pivot**   Rotate.

**pivot joint**   A joint that allows rotation, such as where the skull is connected to the spine.

**plane**   A flat surface.

**planet**   A body that revolves around a sun and shines only by the light it reflects.

**plasma**   The liquid part of blood in which blood cells are suspended.

**plasticity**   The condition of a substance that is in between the liquid and solid phase.

**Polaris**   The North Star; the star that the north end of Earth's axis points toward.

**pollen grains**   Cells that form sperm.

**pollen tube**   Long tube that grows from a pollen grain down the style of a flower to the ovule through which sperm move to reach the eggs in an ovule.

**pollination**   The transfer of pollen grains from the anther to the stigma.

**positive terminal**   A terminal with a positive charge.

**potential energy (PE)**   The energy of position or condition of an object that can be changed into kinetic energy.

**prokaryotic cells**   Cells without a nucleus, found in single-cell organisms such as bacteria.

**protein**   The nutrient used for growth and repair.

**proton**   Positively charged particle found inside the nucleus of an atom.

**pulley**   A lever that rotates about a fixed point.

**pupa (plural pupae)**   The third and the resting stage of complete metamorphosis during which the larva changes into an adult.

**qualitative**   Pertaining to the characteristic of something, such as being hot or cold.

**quantitative**   Pertaining to the measuring of the amount of something, such as an exact temperature.

**receptacle**   A plant part between the base of a flower and the end of the pedicel that supports the flower.

**reflecting telescope**   A telescope that uses lenses and mirrors to make distant objects appear closer. Also called a **Newtonian telescope.**

**refracted**   Bent.

**refracting telescope**   A telescope that uses only lenses to make distant objects appear closer.

**relax**   In reference to muscles, it means to lengthen.

**repel**   To push away.

**reproduction**   The process by which new organisms are produced.

**reproductive system**   A system that contains organs for reproduction.

**resistance distance ($d_R$)**   In reference to doing work, it is the distance an object is moved.

**resistance force ($F_R$)**   The force you and the machine are working against.

**respiratory system**   Body parts that work together to help you breathe.

**reverse fault**   A dip-slip fault caused by compression in which the hanging wall moves upward in relation to the footwall.

**revolve**   To move in a curved path around another body, such as the Moon revolving around Earth; to orbit.

**ribosomes**   Tiny structures found free in the cytoplasm or on the surface of rough endoplasmic reticulum. The structure where protein is made.

**right lateral fault**   Relative to an observer standing on one of the fault blocks, it is a lateral fault in which the other block moves to the right.

**rock**   A naturally occurring solid made up of one or more minerals.

**rock cycle**   Changing of rocks from one type to another by a series of processes involving heat, pressure, melting, cooling, and sedimentation.

**rotate**   To turn around an axis, such as the rotation of Earth around its axis.

**rumple**   To crush into wrinkles.

**scale**   A ratio between the measurements of a diagram or a model and the actual measurements of an object.

**scale model**   A replica made in proportion to the object it represents.

**scapula**   A shoulder bone.

**screw**   An inclined plane wrapped around a cylinder forming spiraling ridges; a simple machine.

**season**   One of four divisions of the year—winter, spring, summer, and autumn—characterized by differences in average temperature and in the amount of time that the Sun is in the sky each day.

**sediment**   Loose rock and soil that has been transported by wind, rain, or ice and deposited in another place.

**sedimentary rock**   Rock formed by deposits of sediment.

**seed**   The part of a flowering plant from which a new plant grows.

**sepals**   The leaflike structures that surround and protect a flower before it opens.

**series circuit**   An electric circuit in which there is only one path for the current.

**sexual reproduction**   The forming of a new organism by fertilization.

**shear**   The force that pushes on rocks from different directions, causing them to twist and break.

**shield volcano**   A volcano composed of layers of solidified lava, a wide base, and a large, bowl-shaped opening at the top.

**shiver**   The shaking of muscle due to their being cold.

**shooting star**   A meteor.

**SI (International System)**   The internationally agreed-upon method of using the metric system of measurement.

**silicates**   Chemicals made of the elements silicon and oxygen combined with another element, such as iron and magnesium.

**simple machines**   The most basic machines: inclined plane, wedge, screw, lever, wheel and axle, and pulley.

**skeletal muscles**   Muscles attached to bones.

**slightly movable joints**   Joints with limited motion, such as those attaching the ribs to the spine.

**smooth muscles**   Muscles that form internal organs, such as the lungs; muscles that cause shivering and goosebumps due to being cold.

**solar system**   A sun and all its orbiting celestial bodies.

**solid**   A state of matter. See **amorphous solid** and **crystalline solid.**

**solution**   A mixture that is uniformly blended.

**Southern Hemisphere**   The area south of the equator.

**South Pole**   The south end of Earth's axis.

**south pole**   The end of a magnet attracted to the magnetic south pole of Earth.

**span**   A length measurement equal to the distance from the tip of the thumb to the tip of the little finger of an outstretched hand.

**sperm**   A male reproductive cell.

**spine**   Backbone.

**spring**   The season between winter and summer with warm days and cool nights.

**spring equinox**   The first day of spring, on or about March 22, in the Northern Hemisphere.

**spring scale**   An instrument used to measure the weight of an object.

**stamen**   The male reproductive organ of a flower.

**stars**   Celestial bodies made of gases that are so hot they give off light.

**states of matter**   The forms in which matter exists. The three major states of matter are solid, liquid, and gas.

**static electricity**   The buildup of stationary electric charges.

**stigma**   The sticky top of a carpel that holds pollen grains that land on it.

**stony meteorites**   Meteorites made of material similar to that found in the rocks on Earth's surface.

**stress**   Force.

**strike-slip fault**   See **lateral fault.**

**style**   A tubelike structure in a carpel that supports the stigma and connects it with the ovary.

**substance**   A basic part of matter made of one kind of matter—an element or a compound.

**summer**   The climatic season following spring with hot days and warm nights.

**summer solstice**   The first day of summer, on or about June 22, in the Northern Hemisphere.

**sun**   A star with a group of celestial bodies orbiting it. The name of the star in our solar system is the Sun.

**superior planets**   Planets whose orbit is farther away from the Sun than Earth's orbit; Mars, Jupiter, Saturn, Uranus, Neptune, and Pluto.

**symbol**   In reference to chemicals, letters used to represent an atom of a particular element.

**synovial fluid**   A thick fluid found in joints that reduces friction.

**synthetic elements**   Elements made by scientists in a laboratory, such as californium, plutonium, nobelium, and einsteinium.

**telescope**   An instrument used to make distant objects appear nearer and larger.

**temperate zones**   The two regions between latitudes 23. 5° and 66.5° north and south of the equator.

**temperature**   (1) A measure of how hot or cold an object is. (2) The average kinetic energy of the particles of a material, calculated by dividing the thermal energy by the total number of particles.

**tendon**   A tough, nonelastic tissue that attaches some skeletal muscles to bones.

**tension**   Stretching forces that can be strong enough to pull rocks apart.

**tephra**   Lava blasted into the air by a violent volcanic eruption that solidifies as it falls to the ground.

**terminal**   The point at which a connection is made to an electrical device.

**thermal energy**   The sum of the kinetic energy of all particles making up a material.

**thermometer**   An instrument that measures the temperature of a material.

**third quarter phase**   The moon phase following the full moon in which half of the side of the Moon facing Earth is lighted; the moon phase when three-fourths of a lunar month has passed.

**tissue**   Groups of similar cells with similar functions.

**triceps**   Extensor muscle on the back side of your upper arm; the muscle that lowers the forearm.

**uncia**   A Roman length measurement equal to the width of a man's thumb. There were 12 uncias in 1 foot.

**unicellular**   Made of one cell.

**universe**   Earth and everything else in space.

**vapor**   The gaseous state of a substance, such as water, that is normally in a liquid or solid state.

**vaporizes**   Changes to a gas.

**vertebra**   (plural **vertebrae**) One of the bony structures that make up the spine.

**vertebrate**   An animal with a backbone.

**viscosity**   The measure of how fast a liquid flows.

**volcanic bombs**   Large rocks throughout the vent of a volcano during a violent eruption.

**volcanic eruption**   When lava, ash, debris, and/or gas are thrown out of a volcano.

**volcanic vent**   Pipelike opening in Earth's crust connecting a volcano's crater to the magma chamber.

**volcano**   The mountain or hill formed by the accumulation of materials erupted through one or more openings in Earth's surface.

**volume**   The amount of space an object occupies.

**voluntary muscles** Muscles that can be controlled at will.

**waning**   Getting smaller.

**waxing**   Getting larger.

**weathering**   The process by which rocks are broken into smaller pieces.

**wedge**   An inclined plane that moves; a simple machine.

**weight**   On Earth, it is the measure of the gravitational force of Earth acting on an object.

**wheel and axle**   A lever that rotates in a circle.

**wing pads**   Small winglike growths on nymphs.

**winter**   The season between autumn and spring with cold days and nights.

**winter solstice**   The first day of winter, on or about December 22, in the Northern Hemisphere.

**work**   What is accomplished when a force causes an object to move; the amount of force on an object times the distance the object moves in the direction of the force; the transfer of energy that occurs when a force causes an object to move.

**wrist**   The joint connecting your forearm with your hand.

# Index